Practical Discipleship
in the
Classroom

A Kingdom-building, Heaven-filling
Approach to School Discipline
Based on the Principles of
Biblical Counseling

By

Kerry Dougan

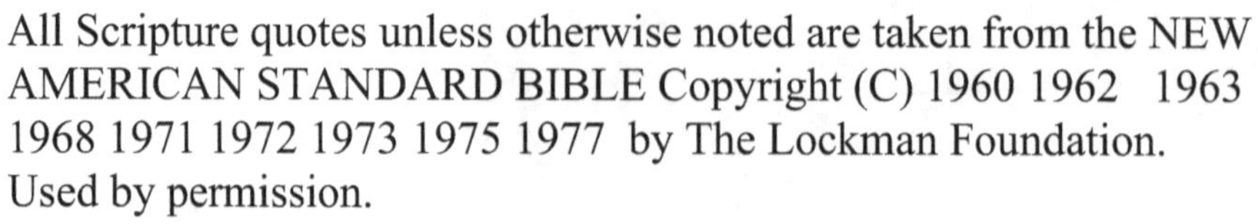

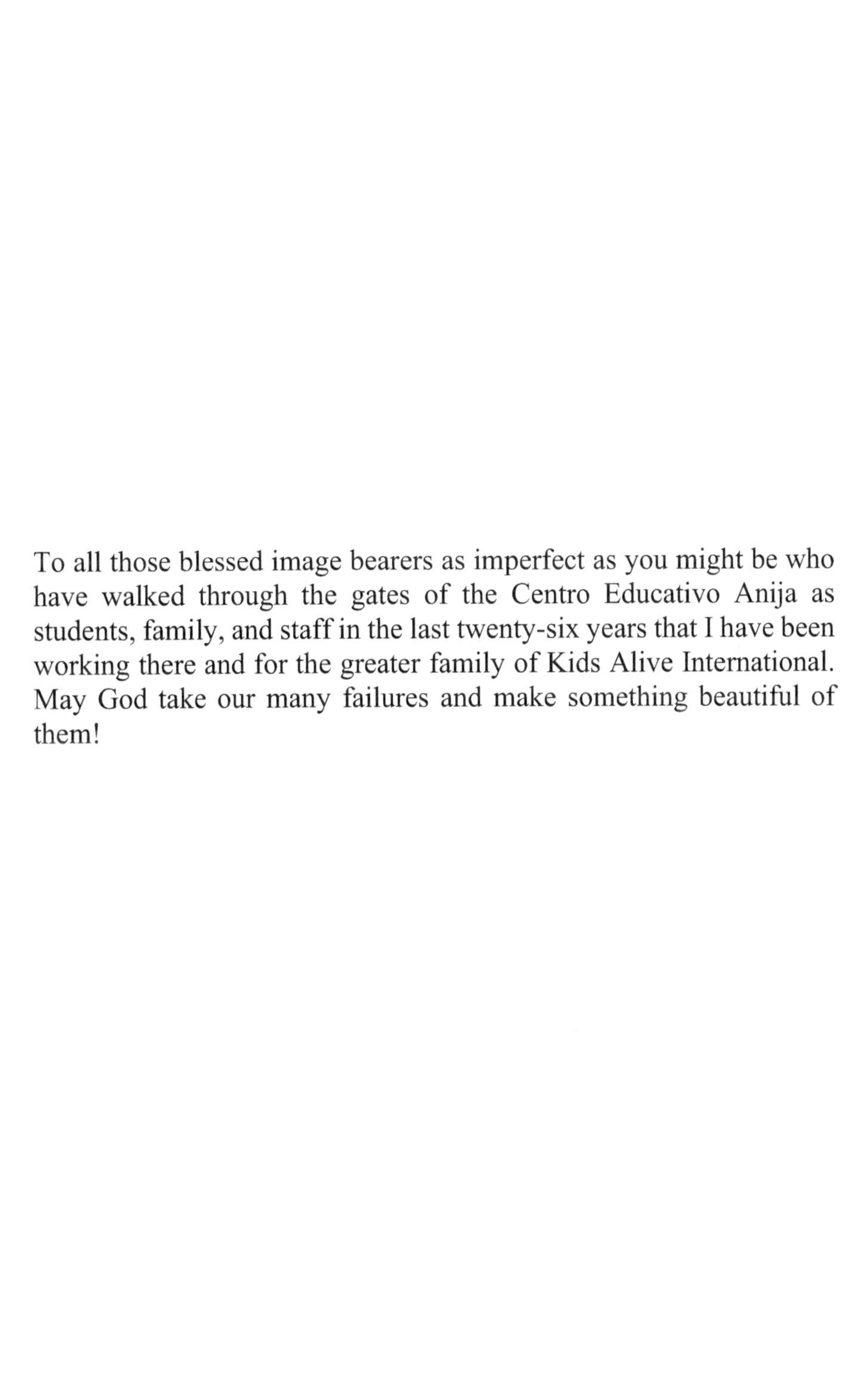

To all those blessed image bearers as imperfect as you might be who have walked through the gates of the Centro Educativo Anija as students, family, and staff in the last twenty-six years that I have been working there and for the greater family of Kids Alive International. May God take our many failures and make something beautiful of them!

Acknowledgments

I wish to thank the entire staff of the Centro Educativo Anija for all the love and support you have given me for the last twenty-six years. It has been a great ride!

Thank you more specifically to Paul Cooper my true comrade in arms who has read this manuscript and provided many helpful insights that have improved the final product significantly.

Thank you to Rómery Serrata my daughter in the faith who is working on my Spanish translation which I hope will make this work available to the many Spanish speakers with whom I wish to share it.

Thank you to my other comrade in arms Josué Marión for your prayers and support. It has been a greater pleasure than I can express to work side-by-side with you.

Thank you to Ann Van Der Molen, Anija principal who has given me the opportunity to share these principles and put up with my sometimes somewhat revolutionary ideas.

Thank you to my wife Milagros who has stood by me through happiness and tears for these nearly twenty-eight years and who has prayed for God's blessing on this book.

Thank you to the many children with whom through trial and error I have learned these principles.

Thank you to the biblical counseling staff at Faith Church in Lafayette IN. You don't know who I am and neither do you know how much you have given me and many others through your biblical counseling training.

Table of Contents

Preface

I sat mesmerized, hanging on every word of the speaker. My mind was being transformed by an old, old friend and the emotional energy that welled up within me was nothing short of ecstasy, an energy that has not diminished up to this day now over a year and a half later.

The date was April 26, 2019, and I was sitting in a training conference on biblical counseling in Santo Domingo, Dominican Republic put on by the visiting team from Faith Church in Lafayette, Indiana. I had come to the conference more from a sense of obligation than one of enthusiasm. I loved the Bible but greatly preferred studying it myself to listening to other people expound it. I am also a classic introvert and a lover of routine order nearly to the point of fanaticism. Even such a thing as a day on the beach makes me cringe, especially if I have to drive to get there, how much more a conference that I had little confidence was going to add one iota to my life!

Nevertheless, here I was, drinking in every word as the sheer raw power of the Bible was laid bare before me. I had always been suspicious of clinical psychology and had debated its value for years. (I have more or less concluded the truth of this, admittedly oversimplified answer—that it may have value as far as methods but has nothing to offer in terms of solutions.) However, I had never contemplated the power of the Word of God to touch every nook and cranny of one's life, particularly in the midst of suffering. To be honest, at 53 years old I had never really yet suffered in life although within a year a family crisis, which I shall not discuss here, would teach me the meaning of suffering.

I have said that my mind was being transformed. My heart had been transformed many, many years before to the point I think the word *transformed* to be a trifle long to describe it. Better said my heart was just formed. I am not one of those Christians who has been converted. Conversion implies you were something else before you were the thing you were converted to. If one feels that being converted from an infant to a Christian is a fair use of the word then I shall not argue, but it is not a use I would make of it. I have simply been a Christian as long as I have been capable of understanding—since I was a very small child. After all, Christ offers a dire warning to those who would cause one of these little ones *who believe in me* to stumble. For many of *these little ones* perhaps their natural child's belief does not mature into a saving faith. I have seen that to be an all-too-painful reality. However, in my life it did. I simply grew from an infant human being and Christian on both a physical and spiritual milk diet to a healthy meat-eating adult. That is I!

I have called the Bible an old, old friend. When I was a child, I memorized every Bible story I ever heard such that I was rather well known in my church for correcting the pastor at a very young age. I received my first Bible from my church when I was seven, a King James version, and another, a Living Bible, from my grandmother upon my baptism a few months later. I immediately began to devour it. I determined that I would dedicate one day a week to reading the Bible, and that was what I did. I would not touch the Bible Monday through Friday, but even at seven or eight years of age I sat down on Saturday and literally read it for the entire day, morning to evening. Simple math says I must have gone about that for around three months because I remember reading between thirty and forty chapters a day, and I died in Psalms. That book was just too dull for my young mind. I did eventually pick the Bible back up and finished reading through it for the first time when I was in 5th grade. I remember clearly because I petitioned my teacher to allow me to do a book report on it. She refused, and, honestly, I understand. After all, how do you do a book report on the entire Bible? Maybe it would work for the book of Matthew, the book of 2 Kings, or of Ezekiel, but of the entire Bible? It was fine; I far exceeded my reading expectation anyway!

Still despite my love for the Bible, I viewed it mostly as an intellectual pursuit. I knew it taught certain principles which I was anxious to keep, but I understood these to be quite simple and straight forward. I enjoyed the stories, but I never viewed the Bible as having answers to life's particularly complex questions. That may have been partly due to the fact that my life in itself was fairly simple, and I had never experienced hardship. I didn't see much need for that kind of help on a personal level and didn't understand others' need for it. Beyond that, while I very much credit my parents as the primary earthly instruments through which the Lord brought me to Himself, we seldom opened the Bible as a family. I never remember them sharing its truth with me when discipline was in order or at any other time except in church which we faithfully attended.

My eyes were opened somewhat in my early high school years. A godly man of the church held a Wednesday night Bible study which some four or five youth attended. Now this man probably would not have won any awards for the best Bible study—it seems to me he arrived many days with no particular plan—but he would listen to us and to all our struggles and then he would say: *Well let's see what the Bible has to say about that.* It was the first time I had ever seen anyone who actually consulted the Bible for matters concerning his own everyday life, and it made an impression on me. Several of my favorite verses including Titus 1:15 and John 15:15 I discovered during this time. To this day I consider this man to have been the only true mentor I have ever had in my Christian walk.

Even so, I still had no true appreciation for the raw power of the gospel to change lives. After getting my undergraduate degree in chemical engineering from Purdue University, coincidentally right across the Wabash from Lafayette, IN, I worked in a steel mill on the Indiana lake shore for six years before answering God's call to the mission field. I was led to the mountains of the central Dominican Republic to a small town called Jarabacoa where I met my wife and where we have now served for 25 years. We work at a mission called Kids Alive International which administers orphanages and schools for at-risk children around the world. I held various different functions within our school called the Centro Educativo Anija (a Spanish acronym which means helping children of Jarabacoa), but eventually I took the position of assistant principle in charge of discipline. Now the previous individuals charged with that roll really had not figured it out. I came really knowing little more than they but with more of a willingness to try new things, and thus began my gradually improving process of trial and error that led up to that day that I sat in that conference on biblical counseling. And now in the midst of this conference I had had little desire to actually attend, my head was swimming with possibilities as to what this would mean to my job and my school.

After the conference, I returned home to Jarabacoa and began applying all I had learned, and I immediately began seeing fruit. I saw some beautiful things like the young middle school kid who asked me one day how I saw his Christian walk. The very fact he would ask that question says a lot about who he was, and although he was a kid prone to get himself into considerable trouble at times, I've never seen anyone that listens so attentively to biblical correction and later prays it all back to God in repentance. Then there was the other middle schooler, also prone to discipline problems, who asked me for a Bible and once he had received it, has hardly let it out of his sight. Then there was the high school girl who came up to me with an urgent look in her eyes and told me *Kerry I need you to pray for me. I just had a terrible thought that doesn't please God.* I don't know what the thought was but the fact she thought enough to ask for prayer for a sin which no one even knew about spoke volumes.

Still, as time went by our mission began introducing new discipline methods often developed upon worldly foundations. We had years earlier placed in our school's constitution a clause that defined the three purposes of discipline in order of importance as evangelism, sanctification, and producing an effective learning environment. We had always stated it, but we had never taught it. We really hadn't known how! It was something I and my counselors were beginning to understand, but something of which most of our teachers had not the slightest inclination, and so they drank in the words of any new discipline technique, incapable of placing it on its proper foundation, the Word of God. So how could we teach them? I had no idea!

I began to read avidly the works of the great biblical counselors, particularly Jay Adams and many others, but though these principles seemed made for Christian school discipline, no one that I could find seemed to have applied them in writing to that setting in a practical way. The best I could find was Paul Tripp, but he left me dissatisfied for two major reasons. First, although his principles are all very biblical, he tends to make far less use of the Bible than I like to see. One can read chapters of his books with only a passing reference to a Bible verse. Second his ideas seem to remain primarily in the range of theory and seldom get down to rough and tumble techniques for sealing with real disciplinary situations.

All through that following year, I anxiously awaited the return of the folks from Lafayette to the conference. Excitedly, I signed up some thirty people from my mission to attend, but alas, due to the proximity to the elections, the conference was canceled for that year. It was just as well, as had not the elections, COVID 19 would certainly have canceled it anyway. As it was, it was canceled early enough that I was able take advantage of an opportunity to take the conference a little bit earlier in February of 2020 in the very epicenter of the biblical counseling world, Lafayette, Indiana. Surely there in Lafayette I could get my answers!

Well, the conference met or exceeded my now-very-high expectations, but still I heard very little that would lead me as to how to apply the principles to school discipline. I even voiced my desire to one of the conference leaders who simply asked: *Why would biblical counseling be any different in a school setting than it is in any other?* Why indeed? He didn't get it. In the vast resource room with literally thousands of books all dedicated to biblical counseling themes, I only found one which somewhat tangentially dealt with an educational setting. That book spoke more specifically of ADHD diagnoses. I bought it and devoured it, and I did find some gems within it, but I found nothing close to a comprehensive approach to discipline in the classroom.

Still, I held out hope. I knew that the folks from Lafayette also ran a Christian school. It was my plan to return to the States that following summer and visit that school in Lafayette to learn what I could. Alas, it was not to be. COVID 19 hit, and I was forced to stay in the Dominican. My trip back to the States has been delayed perhaps up to two years, and I simply could not wait that long. Shut in my own home for weeks and months on end with nothing else to do, I decided to take up Jay Adams' challenge. In his *Lectures on Counseling* he asks and answers the question concerning the young man desiring to take up the mantle of a truly biblical counselor in his ministry:

> Since almost all of the resources available are either meagre, superficial, or erroneous what must he do? The answer is that he must do a lot of his own spade work. Since there is little for him to rely upon, he must break much new ground himself. That is the crux of what I have to say today. He will waste his time leaning on the bent reeds of the past. He finds that they snap under the weight of serious pastoral concern. Instead, he must saturate himself with the Scriptures to discover there what God says about life on this planet as well as life in the age to come. He must break up the clods and dig out the stones himself if he really wants to become a biblical counselor. He must tap the rich

reservoirs of biblical truth lying offshore from the mainland operations that are now petering out.

This is where I have found myself. Certainly by now Adams and his many followers have effectively broken up the clods of biblical counseling and provided a myriad of resources to the individual who desires to invest himself in that pursuit. However, applying that method to a classroom situation is another thing. This book is my feeble attempt to do my own spadework and create a model of scholastic discipline planted firmly over the foundation of the Holy Scriptures. In this spirit I submit to you the present work. Far from the last word on discipline based on the principles of biblical counseling, it is my hope that this is only the first, and that others far more capable will write the far greater works that undoubtedly could be written on the topic. Still, feeble though I may be, I know that when you build squarely on the Word of God, you can hardly go wrong. Let us begin then our study of Practical Discipleship in the Christian Classroom.

I. Three Words to Light the Way

The Breadth of Classroom Discipline and the Focus of our Book

In any disciplinary policy there are three main points of attack the proactive, the reactive, and the reactive-proactive.

Now the proactive point of disciplinary policy focuses on preventing problems and involves literally everything we do within the school which does not fall into the other two categories. Good lesson plans are devised to engage a child's attention and maintain order. Classroom rules and routines are devised so that children may understand and follow the teacher's expectations. Meeting a child's physical needs such as providing food and water for him are attempts to make him comfortable and avoid problems. Recess allows a child a healthy outlet to blow off steam so as to help him focus during the time he is in class. We teach Bible purity and Peacemakers classes to train a child in the way he should go. We teach our students to respond to certain value phrases also. Even such details as keeping the floors clean and the way we arrange the desks have to do with creating an orderly environment in which real learning may take place.

Despite all these preparations, problems will and do occur. After all, we cannot control the difficulties children bring from home (although we may influence them), and even if we could, we as teachers have problems and shortcomings of our own. Even though we have heard it a hundred times from our pulpits, it is never correct to call a Christian a sinner since he has a new identity in Christ. I've often explained it to my students by asking them how many of them do not consider themselves soccer players. Soccer is huge in Jarabacoa and ninety percent of my students *do* consider themselves soccer players. Still invariably someone will raise his hand. To this student I will ask *You mean you never play soccer?* No of course he has played and continues to play. You could hardly attend our school otherwise. Still he does not identify himself as a soccer player because soccer simply is not part of his nature. It is not part of who he truly is. When he plays soccer, he is doing something contrary to who he feels himself to be. In the same way we as Christians may and often do sin. A sinner sins because he is a sinner, but a Christian sins contrary to his true nature. He is not properly called a sinner. This concept is really quite biblical. Yes, the Bible says that all have sinned, but it never uses the term *sinner* to describe an individual bought and transformed by the blood of Christ. Still, although we are no longer sinners as I have implied, none among us have realized our complete liberation from that old sinful nature as of yet. The result is that the best proactive discipline plan conceivable by man and dare I say even by God in our fallen world is incapable of producing a problemless environment. After all, Adam and Eve sinned even in the perfect environment of the Garden of Eden. Thus we must develop a plan for reactive discipline. This is composed of the procedures we follow after a problem has occurred. It includes counseling meetings with parents and consequences up to and including suspensions and expulsions.

Finally the reactive-proactive portion of our discipline plan is that part in which we attempt to learn from the past patterns of poor conduct and apply that knowledge to diminish these patterns and prevent similar conduct in the future.

Since the proactive area of discipline covers literally everything we do in school, it does not fall within the scope of this work to speak of these things. We will rather focus on the last two points of attack, the reactive and reactive-proactive areas of discipline.

The Purpose of Classroom Discipline

To begin our journey toward biblical classroom discipline, we must answer this fundamental question. Just what is its purpose? Would it surprise you to know that the purpose of classroom discipline in a Christian school is quite different than in a secular school? It certainly ought to be. The school in which I serve is called the Centro Educativo Anija. (Anija is a Spanish acronym for helping children of Jarabacoa, our town in the central Dominican Republic.) Our foundational document states the following about school discipline:

The three purposes for discipline in order of importance are:

1) To open the child's eyes to the reality of sin and to his need of a Savior.
2) To mold a child to the image of Christ.
3) To eliminate barriers to an environment that facilitates learning. *(translated by the author from the original Spanish)*

Now there is nothing precisely inspired about this description but it is to be hoped that no Christian school would dispute it. Assuming this, we might make two observations about this statement. First of all, while we declare purpose number three the least important, subject as we are to normal human weaknesses, we may often unwittingly, in the passion of the moment, act as if it were the most important. If this is true of us, how much more so of public-school teachers! In the public school, purpose number three is without a doubt the primary focus in their disciplinary philosophy, if not always in word definitely in practice. If they go at all beyond this in their documents it may be to cite such noble-sounding goals as to form the child as a loyal citizen of his country and a productive member of society. Still, the focus of the Christian school should be quite different, and there may be no other place where this difference is better evidenced than in its disciplinary philosophy expressed in our school in goals number 1 and 2. These two goals may be summed up in one word each, evangelism and discipleship, which have for their ends salvation and sanctification. It is the purpose and goal of discipline in a Christian school to see the child saved and to further the process of his sanctification. In our school, also, we have a motto: *Educating for Eternal Life*. A Christian school ought by all means to look beyond worldly goals to those that transcend this lifetime. This is the very reason for its existence.

Therefore, throughout the rest of this book, we shall use a different term for discipline. While historically the word *discipline* carried exactly the meaning we desire for it, the truth is that in our modern society the word has become degraded to signify primarily the application of negative consequences for inappropriate behavior. The true meaning goes far beyond that, but to avoid confusion we shall use a related term. Discipline for us should be the application of biblical principles to the circumstances of everyday life. It is training a child to live biblically, and there is no term that better communicates our meaning to the modern mind than *practical discipleship*.

The second observation is the absolute audacity of the second goal. To mold a child to the image of Christ? Is that even within our power? Of course it isn't! Then how dare we make that a goal? In the climax of the Tim Burton movie *Alice in Wonderland*, on the Frabulous Day as the Jabberwock comes out to meet Alice in the final showdown, the monster growls: "So my old foe, we meet on the battlefield once again." "We've never met," counters Alice. "Not you, you insignificant girl," roars the Jabberwock, "my ancient enemy the Vorpal Sword!" The ability to defeat the Jabberwock does not reside in any power that Alice might hold; it resides completely in the weapon she wields. In the same way our audaciousness in declaring the purpose and goal of our disciplinary strategy to form a child in the image of Christ is based not on any human virtue we may even aspire to. It is based on the weapon we wield, the power of the written Word of God. After all *faith comes from hearing and hearing by the word of Christ.* (Romans 10:17) Also *the word of God is living and active and sharper than any two-edged sword and piercing as far as the division of soul and spirit of both joints and marrow and able to judge the thoughts and intentions of the heart.* (Hebrews 4:12) Would Alice dare to fight the Jabberwock without the Vorpal Sword in her hand? How can we Christians dare to fight the devil without the Word of God? How can we as Christian educators dare to declare that our purpose in applying discipline is to form a child into the image of God without using the one weapon that actually has the power to do it?

But Can Children be Biblically Counseled?

If the answer to this question seems painfully obvious to you then you are probably not aware of one of the central principles of biblical counseling: You cannot counsel an unbeliever. Unbelievers can hardly be expected to be taught from a book that they do not accept. They must first be evangelized. However, does this principle hold true with children?

It must be said to start out that no absolutely universal answer may be given to this question. Though we may cite general truths for most children, we cannot proclaim a truth that applies to every child we have ever met.

Nevertheless, I have come to the conclusion that while their unbelieving parents could never receive biblical counseling, most children can and should receive it. Unbelieving adults have either actively rejected God's Word or have not felt it worthy of their attention. Children, however, have not yet developed a cosmovision that is contrary to Christianity. Their minds need only be formed and not *re*formed or *trans*formed. They usually have not actively rejected the Word of God, and while they may not yet have what we may call a saving faith, they do, nevertheless, have a natural child's faith that imparts a certain protective grace over their otherwise vulnerable hearts. This principle is born out in Scripture.

Let us consider the first six verses of Matthew 18:

> **At that time the disciples came to Jesus and said, "Who then is greatest in the kingdom of heaven?"** [2] **And He called a child to Himself and set him before them** [3] **and said, "Truly I say to you unless you are converted and become like children, you will not enter the kingdom of heaven.** [4] **Whoever then humbles himself as this child, he is the greatest in the kingdom of heaven.** [5] **And whoever receives one such child in My name receives me;** [6] **but whoever causes one of these little ones who believe in Me to stumble, it would be better for him to have a heavy millstone hung around his neck and to be drowned in the depth of the sea.**

The first observation we may make concerning this passage is that childhood is held up as an example of faith and humility to follow if one wants even to *see* the kingdom of heaven. Interpretation? Children are naturally closer to God than their adult counterparts. The second observation is based on the words of verse six*: but whoever causes one of these little ones **who believe in Me** to stumble...* Clearly, Christ is teaching us here that while the natural state of a man is unbelief, the natural state of a child is belief, and truly the children *did* believe in Jesus just as the young boy who was foolish enough to think that Jesus could do something great with his lunch and went on to see that lunch his mother had lovingly packed for him feed 5000 men and their families. Certainly, children are naturally credulous and easily believe terrible lies, but if you teach them of the love of God, they will naturally believe that until someone gives them reason not to, or until they obtain that adult skepticism that comes with age.

Another key scripture is found in 1 Corinthians 7 in a discussion of the responsibilities of those Christian spouses who find themselves unequally yoked in marriage to unbelievers. Paul calls them very clearly to remain with their spouses if those spouses are willing. Verse 14 is of great interest here: *For the unbelieving husband is sanctified through his wife and the unbelieving wife is sanctified through her believing husband; for otherwise your children are unclean, but now they are holy.* What a fascinating statement! An unbelieving husband or wife is somehow sanctified by his or her spouse, *and their children are holy!* Now we may speculate as to exactly what that means, but we *must* understand that the children of even one saved parent are covered in some way by a special grace. Might not a similar grace apply to those who are enrolled in Christian schools, though they come from unbelieving homes? After all, the very meaning of the word *holy* is *set apart.* Are not children very much set apart by the fact they attend a Christian school? Beyond this I cannot point to a scripture that supports this concept specifically in the context of Christian schools but I do believe that such a grace is granted to those children chosen out of the world to attend. I have worked in a Christian school for at-risk children for over 25 years. Highly unusual among Christian schools, the great majority of our children come from non-Christian homes, and I have seen this principle manifested in each student I have worked with.

In the end then in most cases, it *is* altogether correct to use biblical counseling for children.

Three Words to Guide Us

To develop a model of practical discipleship in the classroom based on the principles of biblical counseling, the first question we must answer is: What exactly is the role of the teacher? Jay Adams, the undisputed father of the modern biblical counseling movement, has produced, in his long lifetime, an enormous volume of literature to serve as support for the biblical counselor. The term Adams used to name his new school was *nouthetic counseling.* Indeed, he even fixed this name to the biblical counseling society that sprang up among his followers; but just what does this word mean?

The word *nouthetic* is a transliterated adjective form of the Greek verb *νουθετεω (noutheteo).* It is a compound of the words *nous,* translated *mind* or *understanding,* and *theteo,* which means *to orient* or *to fix in position. Noutheteo,* then, means *to fix in the mind.* It is usually translated *to admonish* or at times *to warn.* It seemed a perfect word to distinguish Adams's form of counseling from all others because it centers on sin as the central cause of human suffering.

Adams's early experience as a disciple of Orval Hobart Mowrer led him to understand the human need for repentance. Mowrer had grown up as a conservative Christian, and, although he abandoned the faith at a fairly young age, he was later influenced in his work by various Christian authors. This influence, while never completely convincing him of Christianity's deeper truths, did lead him to reject Freud's belief that psychological problems were caused by imagined guilt. Mowrer understood that guilt to be all too real! His integrity groups were developed to encourage people to form a lifetime commitment to honesty and confession of their innermost sins, and while they lasted, they enjoyed a remarkable success rate among his patients. Still, with his death, integrity groups passed into history, but much of Mowrer's theory and practice was successfully adopted into drug and alcohol rehabilitation programs that continue to this day. They also impressed his protégé, Jay Adams, but the young Christian also understood the shortcomings of his teacher's theories. Mowrer had not taken into consideration a person's need for reconciliation with his God, a truth which, in the end, would have far greater consequences upon his life than his relationships with other people. To Adams, *noutheteo* appeared to represent very well the heart of biblical counseling.

Several times, *noutheteo* is presented as a Christian responsibility we all have one to another. In Romans 15:14 we see: *And concerning you, my brethren, I myself also am convinced that you yourselves are full of goodness, filled with all knowledge, and able also to admonish* (noutheteo) *one another.* Colossians 3:16 emphasizes the centrality of the word to Christian life as we are commanded to: *Let the word of Christ richly dwell within you with all wisdom, teaching and admonishing* (noutheteo) *one another with psalms and hymns and spiritual songs, singing with thankfulness in your hearts to God.* In 1 Thessalonians 5:14 we are commanded to: *admonish* (noutheteo) *the unruly, encourage the fainthearted, help the weak, be patient with everyone.* Finally, Paul gives us a grave warning in 2 Thessalonians 3:14-15: *If anyone does not obey our instruction in this letter, take special note of that person, and do not associate with him so that he will be put to shame. Yet, do not regard him as an enemy, but admonish* (noutheteo) *him as a brother.*

However, Adams's characterization of biblical counseling with the word *nouthetic* falls a little short. It may be truly said that the origin of every single human struggle may be traced to sin, but that sin has three sources; one's own sin, the sin of those around him, and original sin. The word *noutheteo* truly only fairly represents problems that arise from the first of these sources. Many problems arise from the other two as well for which one need not repent and over which one has no control. Domestic abuse, wars, and horrible crimes of which they were victims have dominated the lives of far too many people. Others have had to deal with the results of natural tragedies like earthquakes or tidal waves or cancer or some other sickness which are a result of living in a sinful world but of no particular sin of theirs or anyone else's. How can we characterize *these* situations?

Christian counselor Robert Kelleman, touted by some as the natural successor to Adams, while affirming the importance of *noutheteo* suggests another word, παρακαλεω (*parakaleo*). Now *parakaleo* is much more common in the New Testament than *noutheteo*. It is a compound of the preposition *para,* which means *beside,* and the verb *kaleo,* which means *to call;* so *parakaleo* literally means *to call alongside.* However, its translations are just about as numerous as the sand of the seashore even within a single version of the Bible. In the New American Standard Bible it is translated *to comfort* on a number of occasions, most notably in the opening chapters of 2 Corinthians when Paul speaks of being comforted in his tribulations. It is also translated *to urge* many times, particularly where Paul over and over urges his readers to some kind of godly action. It is often translated *to exhort* as in Acts 2:40 where Peter exhorts the crowds at Pentecost. It is translated *to invite* in Acts 8:31 when the Ethiopian eunuch invited Philip to climb up and sit with him.

It is translated *to encourage* in a number of places such as Acts 11:23 speaking of Barnabas encouraging the church in Antioch to remain true to the Lord. To muddy the waters even further, the word *parakleto,* which means *one who parakaleo,* appears only five times in the New Testament. (I shall use the English conformed spelling *paraclete* from now on for this term.) Four times it appears in John 14-16 in reference to the Holy Spirit that the Father would send after Jesus' death and is translated *Helper* in the New American Standard and *Counselor* in the Holman Christian Standard. The word also appears in 1 John 2:1 with reference to Jesus Christ and is translated *Advocate* in most versions of the Bible. *My little children, I am writing these things to you so that you may not sin. And if anyone sins, we have an Advocate with the Father, Jesus Christ the righteous.* Beyond that, Barnabas is called in Acts 4:36 the son of *parakleseos,* which is translated *encouragement.*

Truly, it is a challenge to pin down the meaning of this illusive word. However, when we look at some of its more practical uses where it is translated in still other ways, the meaning begins to come into focus. The word is translated *to implore* in Mark 5:23 when Jairus came to implore Jesus to heal his daughter. It is translated *to plead* in Matthew 18:29 in the parable of the two debtors when the first debtor pled with the king to have patience with him in paying his enormous debt. It is translated *to appeal* in Acts 16:9 when Paul has a dream of a man from Macedonia appealing to him to come and help them. Finally it is translated *to entreat* in Matthew 8:31 when the demons Legion entreated Jesus to send them into the herd of swine. Thus, we begin to see a pattern emerge which helps us understand all the previous uses. *Parakaleo* refers, in each and every case, to a communication designed to move others to action. Perhaps the best English translation for the word might be *to motivate.*

This should give us a whole new insight as to what the word *to comfort* means as a translation for *parakaleo.* Comforting one another is not just to make one another feel better. It is to motivate one another to continue actively pressing on, despite difficulties. The Holy Spirit was sent as God's paraclete to motivate us to action while Jesus Christ is our paraclete to move the Father to act on our behalf. Barnabas's power as a paraclete is manifested twice, when he sold a piece of land and lay the price at the feet of the apostles motivating many others to do the same, and when he moved the church of

Jerusalem to receive the recently-converted Saul into fellowship when their instinct was to run and hide.

Perhaps the best image that we might set forth to describe the work of a paraclete is that of a coach preparing his team for the big game. He is a man dedicated to bringing out the best in his players. He is one who stands with them and motivates them to accomplish things seemingly beyond their reach. He defends them, and he also admonishes them when they need it, but no athlete ever hates any true coach because he knows that, in everything, his coach believes in him and wishes to inspire the best in him. As Christian school teachers, this is the image we should have of our role in the lives of our students: that of a coach who stands with them, motivates them, and counts it a personal success when they achieve their goals. The game for which we are coaching is life itself and a life that extends far beyond the limited boundaries of this present reality.

Now *parakaleo* is something we are commanded to over and over in the Scriptures. One of the most salient examples is Titus 1:9 where Paul gives the qualifications of an elder of the church. The elder was to be a teacher that should always be *holding fast the faithful word which is in accordance with the teaching so that he will be able both to exhort* (parakaleo) *in sound doctrine and to refute those who contradict.* One of these church teachers' most important abilities is to *exhort in sound doctrine.* And this he obtains by *holding fast the faithful word* that is the Word of God. As for these teachers within the church, is this surely not also the responsibility of Christian school teachers?

Otherwise, Hebrews 3:13 tells us: *But encourage* (parakaleo) *one another day after day as long as it is still called "Today" so that none of you will be hardened by the deceitfulness of sin.* Also 1 Thessalonians 5:11 tells us: *Therefore, encourage* (parakaleo) *one another and build up one another just as you also are doing.* In a more specific situation after the Corinthians dealt with a sinful member, Paul exhorts them in 2 Corinthians 2:6-8: *Sufficient for such a one is this punishment which was inflicted by the majority so that on the contrary you should rather forgive and comfort* (parakaleo) *him, otherwise such a one might be overwhelmed by excessive sorrow. Wherefore, I urge you to reaffirm your love for him.* In Hebrews 10:24-25 we are commanded: *and let us consider how to stimulate one another to love and good deeds,* [25]*not forsaking our own assembling together as is the habit of some, but encouraging* (parakaleo) *one another; and all the more as you see the day drawing near.* Finally, after a vivid presentation of Christ's future return, Paul commands us in 1 Thessalonians 4:18: *Therefore, comfort* (parakaleo) *one another with these words.* Thereby Paul emphasizes how the act of *parakaleo* has an other-worldly dimension to it. We motivate to action based on our future hope.

In addition to this, we have the example of Paul exhorting and coaching his readers to one good work or another time after time. In the verse listed above of 1 Thessalonians 5:14 Paul urges (parakaleo) us to: *admonish* (noutheteo) *the unruly, encourage the fainthearted, help the weak, be patient with everyone.* (Incidentally here the word *encourage* is not translated from parakaleo.) In Romans 12:1 he tells us: *Therefore, I urge* (parakaleo) *you, brethren, by the mercies of God, to present your bodies a living and holy sacrifice, acceptable to God which is your spiritual service of worship.* In 1 Corinthians 1:10 Paul says: *Now I exhort* (parakaleo) *you, brethren, by the name of our Lord Jesus Christ, that you all agree, and that there be no divisions among you, but that you be made complete in the same mind and in the same judgment.* In the passage we studied above from 2 Corinthians 2:6-8 where Paul pleads with the church to receive once again the expelled sinner, he tells us: *Sufficient for such a one is this punishment which was inflicted by the majority so that on the contrary you should rather forgive and comfort* (parakaleo) *him, otherwise such a one might be overwhelmed by excessive sorrow. Wherefore, I urge* (also parakaleo) *you to reaffirm your love for him.* Finally, in 2 Thessalonians 3:11-12 Paul says: *For we hear that some among you are leading an undisciplined life, doing no work at all but acting like busybodies. Now such persons we command and exhort* (parakaleo) *in the Lord Jesus Christ to work in quiet fashion and eat their own bread.* Many other examples might be presented. Ought not likewise we, as Christian school teachers, continually stand beside our students motivating and urging them forward to all kinds of good works?

The third word to guide us is one which is more specific to our chosen vocation. It is the word διδασκο *(didasko),* translated *to teach.* Now the word *noutheteo* and its related forms are actually found only some 11 times in the entire New Testament. *Parakaleo* and its related forms are found 124 different times in the New

Testament, but *didasko* and its related forms are found some 201 times in the New Testament often in its noun form, *teacher,* a title often given to Jesus.

One of the most pertinent uses of the word *didasko* is found in the Great Commission of Matthew 28:19-20: *Go therefore and make disciples of all the nations, baptizing them in the name of the Father and the Son and the Holy Spirit, teaching* (didasko) *them to observe all that I commanded you; and lo I am with you always, even to the end of the age.* Thus we see that teaching is a central part of Christ's commission to all believers. At the same time the author of Hebrews in chapter 5 verse 12 gives the following rebuke to his readers: *For though by this time you ought to be teachers* (didaskalos), *you have need again for someone to teach* (didasko) *you the elementary principles of the oracles of God, and you have come to need milk and not solid food.* And James strictly warns us in 3:1: *Let not many of you become teachers* (didaskalos), *my brethren, knowing that as such we will incur a stricter judgment.* We shall have much more to say about this warning in chapter 8.

We may conclude that, although we are all called to teach, to be a teacher is a special vocation which not all should aspire to. Further, the Christian school teacher has a much loftier responsibility than her secular counterpart. For the secular teacher, it is quite enough to be highly competent in mathematics and language. But the Christian school teacher must struggle always to be worthy of the high calling she has received. A newly minted Christian is not ready to teach in a Christian school. However it is very clear that many Christian schools do not have high spiritual entrance standards for their teachers and seldom measure their biblical knowledge as a condition to employment. This is a shame, although it may be understandable. Still, although many Christian school teachers may be employed woefully unprepared biblically, this condition must not be allowed to remain as it is. The Christian school teacher must be a constant consumer of the meat of the Word of God so that she might produce milk enough to nourish her disciples, for that is precisely what her students should be to her.

Thus, we see that a Christian school teacher must develop a method of counseling her students that is nouthetic, paracletic, and didactic. It is her purpose to admonish, motivate, and instruct.

Reflection: Consider some concrete ways in which you have used *noutheteo,* admonishment, *parakaleo,* motivation, *and didasko,* teaching in disciplinary cases in the past. Think of some situations where you might have done better. If you are studying this together in a group discuss your reflections. Then write down your thoughts in a personal journal. Think of a practical way to improve in these three areas.

II. Biblical Counseling vs. Psychology

Alternatives to Biblical Counseling

The world offers about as many solutions to man's problems as there are psychologists and psychiatrists who give them, and many of these varied solutions are contradictory. Medical doctors and engineers and scientists of all kinds are generally in agreement about the correct procedures to resolve certain problems and can often do so very successfully to the extent their science has advanced. For any given disease, most doctors would recommend similar procedures to remedy it. To build similar buildings, most engineers would apply similar support structure. Most auto mechanics would provide similar services to correct similar problems with any two vehicles. However, in the world of psychology things are quite different. There is no consensus as to how to deal with life's problems, and the difference between one psychologist or psychiatrist and another may be as night and day. We have already discussed one of the best worldly methods, that of Dr. Orval Hobart Mowrer—best because of the Christian influence he obviously displayed. It is entirely appropriate that we look at a few others of the most popular psychological theories extant in the world today. We shall begin at the beginning with the father of modern-day psychoanalysis, Sigmund Freud.

Freud was born in 1856 and died in 1939. Thus, we must begin by recognizing that this today altogether indispensable field was not available to the inhabitants of this earth from the dawn of time until the lifetimes of our grandparents and great grandparents. Freud was born to Hassidic Jewish parents. Thus, his early life was saturated with instruction from the Jewish Scriptures, but as an adult, his religious beliefs became decidedly antagonistic. Religion had served its purpose in history as a suppressor of primal human aggression, but even then, that positive effect rested on the illusion of the supernatural, more specifically on the killing and eating of a revered paternal figure bringing tranquility and peace of mind to its adherents. (As seen in the Catholic eucharis as well as certain aspects of Freud's childhood Judaism.) However, modern-day science had reduced religion to superfluity and a belief in God to obsoletion.

Graduating from his studies of medicine in 1885, his early years were defined by rigorous scientific study of human anatomy, particularly of the brain. Over time, Freud developed a theory in which he divided the human psyche into three parts which reflect the cartoonish image of a person walking through life with a small red devil speaking in one ear and a winged angel in the other. The devil, he called the id, that portion of the psyche that denies rationality and seeks nothing more than immediate pleasure. The super-ego was the angel, the part of us that views the world through a thoroughly moral lens. However, Freud's view of the id and the super-ego more closely resembled a yin and a yang requiring balance than a good and an evil the one to which one ought always turn and the other from which one ought always flee. It was the job of the third division, the ego, the person in the middle, to consider the counsel of the other two and take the ultimate roll of steering between the two extremes.

His own childhood took center stage in Freud's development of his psychological theories. His hostility and jealousy toward his father for his mother led him to interpret those experiences, often in a highly sexualized manner, as the source of problems which arose much later in life. *Unexpressed emotions will never die,* he wrote. *They are buried alive and will come forth later in uglier ways.* It was therefore the job of the psychologist or the psychiatrist to collect data concerning these past events in order to help the ego steer that ship of life between the constantly nagging id and super-ego. Early in his practice, he experimented with hypnosis and cocaine as methods of obtaining his diagnoses before finally deciding that simple open discussion was the most efficient gateway to the human soul. (He himself continued using cocaine throughout his life as an anti-depressant and a treatment for his frequent migraines.)

B. F. Skinner was another of the twentieth centuries most influential thinkers. Born in 1904 his life spanned most of the twentieth century. He died in 1990. Skinner was an author and inventor as well as a psychologist. His initial university studies were in English literature, and it was his hope to become a novelist. It never happened. While working toward his PhD in Harvard he was challenged to make the study of human behavior an experimental science, and this he accomplished, primarily through controlled observations of rats, pigeons, and other animals and projecting his findings onto human beings. His psychological theory, he called Radical Behaviorism, and the basis for it was that all behaviors are molded by the consequences they have rendered in the past. As he manipulated the behavior of his animals by alternately rewarding them with food or punishing them with mild electrical shocks he projected that the world also did such things in a much more complex way to human beings. Thus, bad behavior was a result of misguided reward or punishment. *No one asks how to motivate a baby,* he wrote. *A baby naturally explores everything it can get at unless restraining forces have already been at work. And this tendency doesn't die out; it's wiped out.*

That Skinner could project his research with rodents and birds onto human beings is not surprising in that he himself was an atheist. He rejected religion from an early age after a Christian teacher tried to assuage the fear of hell instilled in him by his grandmother. To an atheist, a human being is reduced to his biological properties—nothing more than a highly evolved animal!

Abraham Maslow was born in 1908 in New York City, the oldest child of immigrant Jewish parents who had fled Kiev, Ukraine from Czarist persecution. He lived until 1970. As he grew to a youth he experienced much persecution and many times was forced to flee rock-throwing anti-Semitic groups. He also came to resent his mother. He later explained: *What I had reacted to was not only her physical appearance, but also her values and world view, her stinginess, her total selfishness, her lack of love for anyone else in the world – even her own husband and children, her narcissism, her Negro prejudice, her exploitation of everyone, her assumption that anyone was wrong who disagreed with her, her lack of friends, her sloppiness and dirtiness...*

Even so Maslow, as religious atheist, believed in the innate goodness and potential of man. Unlike most psychologists who studied the mentally ill, Maslow considered that the key to unlocking human potential was to be found in the extraordinary members of society and he spent his time studying success stories such as that of Albert Einstein. The main obstacles in life were, he concluded, simply not to have one's needs met. *If the only tool you have is a hammer,* he wrote, *you tend to see every problem as a nail.* Success depended on how full one's tool bag was. He developed his famous hierarchy of needs which his disciples later illustrated graphically with Maslow's Pyramid. A person whose most fundamental needs, as illustrated by the base of the pyramid, were not met could hardly be expected to achieve anything in life, and the level of success one obtained was proportional to the level at which they *were* met. Therefore the key to a successful life was simply getting one's needs met as far up the pyramid as was entirely possible. Left out of his hierarchy was any spiritual consideration. As an atheist, Maslow failed to see that mankind's needs go beyond the biological and the social.

Carl Rogers is considered one of the founding fathers of psychotherapy. His life span ran very close to that of Skinner, having been born two years earlier in 1902 and having died three years earlier in 1987. Rogers was born into a Congregationalist family and therefore was exposed to Christianity at an early age. As a student at the University of Wisconsin, he started out studying agriculture but later switched to history and then planned to go into the ministry. However, after a trip to Peking, China for an international Christian conference, he began to doubt his religious convictions. Even though he enrolled in Union Theological Seminary in New York City, his interest in Christianity faded. He considered himself an atheist through much of his early career and later called himself an agnostic. Toward the end of his life, he was said to have once again embraced some form of spirituality, but that is now difficult to verify, and even if true it hardly resembled Christianity.

Rogers, like Maslow, very much believed in the intrinsic goodness and capacity of every human being. Listening was at the heart of his technique. In his person-centered therapy, he acted on the principal that individuals have the potential within themselves to overcome their difficulties and did not need instruction from outside sources. The counselor's job is simply to unlock that potential. He helps the counselee to process her own thoughts by listening and reflecting them back to her, thus enabling her to find her own solution to her problems. *We think we listen* he wrote *but very rarely do we listen with real understanding, true empathy. Yet listening of this very special kind is one of the most potent forces for change that I know.*

The late British satirist Douglas Adams, himself and agnostic, wrote, nevertheless, a hilarious sketch of a Rogerian analyst in his radio series of the *Hitchhiker's Guide to the Galaxy*. In it he describes a race of extraterrestrials called the Vogons whom he identifies as such an unpleasant and ill-humored race that they should never have survived. In his story, a Vogon spaceship captain, in a ridiculous tirade, orders his entire crew executed. Then he instructs his terrified computer to call his brain care specialist, Gag Halfront, upon which ensues the following dialogue:

Gag Halfront:	Oh, hello, Captain Prostetnic. And how are you feeling today?
Captain Prostetnic:	I appear to have wiped out half of my crew.
Gag Halfront:	Oh, you appear to have wiped out half your crew, have you?
Captain Prostetnic:	That's what I said.
Gag Halfront:	So that's what you said, is it?
Captain Prostetnic:	That *is* what I said.
Gag Halfront:	I see, so that *is* what you said, is it?
Captain Prostetnic:	Yes.
Gag Halfront:	So your answer to my question, "That *is* what you said, is it?" is yes.
Captain Prostetnic:	Yes.
Gag Halfront:	I see. Well, this is very interesting!
Captain Prostetnic:	Mr. Halfront, I have just wiped out half my crew!
Gag Halfront:	So you have just wiped out half your crew…
Captain Prostetnic:	YEEEEEEES!
Gag Halfront:	Well this too is very interesting.
Captain Prostetnic:	Well?
Gag Halfront:	I think this is probably perfectly normal behavior for a Vogon. The natural unhealthy channeling of aggressive instincts into acts of senseless violence…
Captain Prostetnic:	That is exactly what you ALWAYS say!!!
Gag Halfront:	Well, I think that is perfectly normal behavior for a psychiatrist! Hah, hah! (jubilantly) We are clearly both very well-adjusted in our mental attitudes today!

Absurd as it is, this hyperbole demonstrates, in many ways, the emptiness of the worldly systems, particularly that of Rogers. Although Adams, as an agnostic, hardly had any answers himself, he could clearly see through the malaise on which modern psychology is built. Captain Prostetnic clearly does *not* have within himself the power to resolve his problems, and the story accentuates the absurdity of the idea that normal behavior is equivalent to good behavior.

Where are we Grounded?

Before we turn our attention to the method this book pretends to expound, let us first consider the four possible sources on which we build our world view. These are intuition, logic, empiricism, and divine revelation. Intuition speaks of emotions or feelings. It is our inner sense as to how things are or how they ought to be. Logic refers to reason. It is our intellectual deduction as to a probable outcome for a given set of circumstances. Empiricism speaks of the scientific method. It arrives at certain conclusions based on the observed laws of nature. Divine revelation hardly needs any introduction. For the Christian it is the sixty-six books of the Old and New Testaments.

Now each of these four sources has its limitations. Divine revelation is truth limited only by the will of the God who does the revealing. Empiricism is truth decipherable upon application of the scientific method. Significantly, although it may be misinterpreted, science does not lie. However, it is incapable of making the moral judgments necessary to successfully guide us through the sea of human society and culture. It gives us all the tools we need to build a reliably functioning airplane, a communication satellite, or a cell phone; it may help us diagnose and cure diseases; and it may even help us predict human behavior; but it has nothing to offer in determining right and wrong. Logic, like the scientific method, does not teach or even suggest a sense of morality. When skillfully applied, it may guide us in our decision by informing us of probable results of our proposed actions, but it has no mechanism for helping us determine which of those possible results are desirable and which are not. It is up to the individual to make that decision, and, in the absence of divine revelation, it is our intuition that will make the choice. Today's valueless, post-modern society denies the existence of absolute truth but it does allow for every individual to intuitively seek his own truth and leaves us with the expectation that in many ways our individual truths should align for common interests that we hold.

Still, it is only as far as we hold interests in common that our truths will align, making warm intuition the most fallible of these four and in the end easily blown to the right or the left by the winds of our unstable emotions.

Now, although I have not yet presented the case for biblical counseling, it should be clear that this method rests solidly on a foundation of divine revelation which, if it is what it claims to be, is absolutely infallible. It should be equally clear that the secular methods we have outlined above of Freud, Skinner, Maslow, and Rogers are not based on divine revelation since each of them denied its very existence. What then are they based on? The scientific method? Clearly the study of psychology rests on a foundation of morality and values, be those what they may, and as much as Skinner might have claimed empirical study, this cannot be because the scientific method is simply not capable of such judgments. Logic, as we have shown, has the same weakness. It remains, then, that these methods are based upon the ever-fallible intuition of their founders and adherents, regardless of any scientific research they may have put into their development. In truth, the biblical name for intuition is the heart. Our modern society encourages us to "follow your heart," and when a tough decision lies before we ask, "What does your heart tell you?" But the Bible says of the heart in Jeremiah 17:9: *The heart is more deceitful than all else and is desperately sick; Who can understand it?* Other translations say that it is desperately wicked!

Let me also, before moving along, make the following disclaimer. I am hardly an expert in modern psychology. I avoided psychology courses like the plague for my entire academic career, so my knowledge of these great psychologists goes little beyond what one can find in Wikipedia. Undoubtedly, I have provided a simplistic and perhaps even at times an uninformed view of each of these theories. Still, it is indisputable that, because each of these men denied divine revelation, the only option left is that they stand on their own intuition. Their entire systems stand or fall based on one man's truth. And just what is to make that man's truth any better than any other man's?

Let us now then turn to the subject at hand. What exactly is the basis for biblical counseling?

The Eight Fundamental Questions of Biblical Counseling

The fundamental problem with all the worldly counseling systems is that they miss the proverbial elephant in the room. We are all going to die! We can, in many cases, put off the day that we face death but we cannot avoid it. It is there, an invisible phantom, haunting our future, knowing that one day we will encounter that ultimate experience of life and be gathered to the great unknown from which none return. Most of our worldly counseling gurus would tell us that there *is* no great unknown, only eternal darkness and unfeelingness, but no one is truly able to speak to that question outside divine revelation as no one has been able to observe and bear witness to what lies beyond. (Although we remain open to the possibility that a chosen few have been given a glimpse in near-death experiences. It is worthy of note that none of these would side with our atheist friends.) Truly it is remarkable that anyone should expect success in aiding his fellow human beings with life's problems without touching upon those questions. Without those answers, no one can hope for anything better than a very temporary fix from her worldly problems, a temporary trip that will distract her from that haunting specter that will someday come to claim her. Only the biblical counselor is bold enough to face these questions head on and impart to his counselee the assurance that there is, after all, meaning to her life.

Let us unveil the elephant in the form of the eight fundamental questions of life. Now I first was acquainted with these questions in Robert Kelleman's fine volume, *Gospel-Centered Counseling*, but it would be unfair to say the Kelleman was the proper author of the questions. He actually spends a large portion of his book developing each one in eight separate chapters. Here we shall be much briefer but present them we must.

1. What is the truth? Where do I find it?

Now I suppose that each counseling system must claim to hold truth, but most would not claim to have answers to these fundamental questions, at least not helpful ones. And if they do claim the truth, that truth comes from within them. Their system allows for no higher source of revelation.

For the biblical counselor, the source of all truth is our God, and it is found in the God-breathed words of the Old and the New Testaments. Now I have said that even divine inspiration is limited by the divine will, so we might properly ask the question if this inspired Word of God is sufficient. Is it not well, or perhaps even necessary, to supplement it with the scientific discoveries of modern psychology and psychiatry? We must first recognize that some mental illnesses are truly illnesses; they have identifiable physical causes such as accidents and diseases such as Alzheimer's, and they can be treated by medical interventions. However, many cases that are diagnosed as illnesses in modern psychology simply do not have physical causes and are defined by their symptoms alone. For these, the Word of God claims to be entirely sufficient.

Second Timothy 3:16-17 tells us: *All Scripture is inspired by God and profitable for teaching, for reproof, for correction, for training in righteousness; so that the man of God may be adequately equipped for every good work.* Note the language toward the end of this passage. Scripture teaching is enough to make its student *adequately equipped for **every** good work.* Nothing is lacking from the Scriptures and nothing therefore need be added to them. Note also the words of Jesus in the upper room in John 15:15: *No longer do I call you slaves, for the slave does not know what his master is doing; but I have called you friends for all things that I have heard from My Father I have made known to you.* Our Lord lived a perfect life. Let us note, therefore, that Jesus states very clearly that He has withheld nothing of the knowledge with which the Father equipped Him. Everything that Jesus had is available to us as well. Later, Jesus said in His prayer for the disciples to His Father (John 17:17): *Sanctify them in the truth; Your word is truth.* His word is sufficient to sanctify us. Finally the author of Hebrews tells us in 4:12: *For the word of God is living and active and sharper than any two-edged sword and piercing as far as the division of soul and spirit of both joints and marrow and able to judge the thoughts and intentions of the heart.* If we believe the Scriptures, we must believe that they are entirely sufficient to lead us through anything this world might throw at us. Truthfully, we have this promise in 1 Corinthians 10:13: *No temptation has overtaken you but such as is common to man; and God* *is faithful who will not allow you to be tempted beyond what you are able, but with the temptation will provide the way of escape also so that you will be able to endure it.* This promise is to be claimed by every believer as his own.

2. Who is God? How can I know Him?

This question essentially asks, is there anyone bigger than I and my fellow weak beings? The world has offered four possible answers to this question: atheism, monotheism, polytheism, and pantheism.

Now polytheism was the answer of our primitive ancestors, and to be fair, is hardly observed by any civilized people today. Their gods were far from perfect, were anything but infallible, omnipotent, or omniscient, and were often at war one with another. In fact, to a large degree, these gods, while much more powerful than their human underlings, were similarly subject to the forces of nature around them, at times even to death!

Pantheism, on the other hand represents the religions of the East, Hinduism and Buddhism, where God is all. Contrary to the monotheistic God who is outside of and separate from the Creation, the pantheist sees God as an impersonal nature force that encompasses all of Creation, and his concept of heaven is to be completely absorbed into and to become one with that nature God.

Of course, it is primarily atheism with which we are doing battle here. This is the concept that God either does not exist or is distant and irrelevant to everyday life.

Now, observing the fruit of each of the above systems, none apart from monotheism is capable of providing any particular moral compass. If atheism is true, then we are all just unguided accidents of nature who, for no particular reason emerged from oblivion and are bound to return there. Pantheism itself exalts and seeks as the ultimate good a complete denial of self such that one's own independent existence is ultimately surrendered. Is this really attractive to some? Polytheism is dominated by gods who can be even more sinful than their human subjects. If pleasing and appeasing the gods is the center of polytheism then which of the conflicting gods do you appeal to? The strongest?

Only monotheism has the chance of answering this question in a satisfactory and wholesome way, but even then, not all monotheists are equal either. Within this system are subsystems of the monolithic God of Islam and the triune God of Christianity. Only the Christian God, in three distinct persons completely united in intent and purpose, provides the possibility of a God of love. The triune God loves, each member the other two, whereas the Islamic God had no one to love before mankind was created.

Who exactly is our God then? We have the entire Bible to answer that question in as full a manner as He has granted, but simply put, our God is omnipotent omniscient and omnipresent. He is both just and merciful. He is love. He exists in the form of three distinct persons: the Father, the Son, and the Holy Spirit. Of these, the Father is the Supreme Governor of the Universe and the Architect of Creation. He is that omnipresent God who governs the movement of the galaxies and the smallest subatomic particles. The Son is subject to the Father and of the same substance but serves as the Agent of Creation and as our Redeemer as we will speak more presently, and the Holy Spirit is our constant Guide, Companion, and Empowerer while we are here on earth.

For our purposes, the very bare necessities of our faith are expressed in Hebrews 11:6: *And without faith it is impossible to please Him, for he who comes to God must believe that He is and that He is a rewarder of those who seek Him.* Thus, in this passage our faith is reduced to these two essential facts: God exists, and God rewards those who diligently seek Him no matter what their woeful past. Therefore, it is our task both to believe this and to seek out a relationship with this God. That is what He desires from us.

3. Who am I? What is my purpose?

As the aforementioned British satirist Douglas Adams would have it, Why are people born? Our friends from the atheistic secular world *do* have an answer to this. We are simply accidents of evolution. We are part of no great plan. Nothing in life has any real purpose, and nothing we do can ever really make any sense or have any true meaning. We are nothing more than the highest form of animal life, and even that we are the highest is debatable. Dare the secularist speak of these things to his counselee? Just who would he help by doing so? He cannot talk about the elephant. If his counselee realized there is an elephant in the room, how could she handle it? No, the secular psychologist can only hope for success by avoiding this question all together, throwing a blindfold over her eyes so she can't see the elephant and distracting her from his cold perception of reality.

On the other hand, the Christian can face this question boldly. We are beings created in the image of the Almighty God who are destined one day to return to Him. What does it mean to be created in God's image? A conquering emperor in those days of yore would build images of himself wherever he governed to remind all to whom it was they owed their allegiance. We ourselves were thus created to be God's living image, not just to remind all of Creation as to who governs, but to actually govern in His stead. Ephesians 2:10 says: *For we are His workmanship created in Christ Jesus for good works which God prepared beforehand so that we would walk in them.* God created us to do good works, and these works shall extend throughout all eternity. It is for this reason we exist, and this is truly enough to sustain us.

We are His image but we are also lowly slaves to this Almighty God. Is it good to be a slave? Most people would recoil at the very question but the answer is not so simple as at first it seems. It depends upon who your master is! When she visited the courts of King Solomon, the queen of Sheba exclaimed in wonder: *It was a true report which I heard in my own land about your words and your wisdom. Nevertheless I did not believe the reports until I came and my eyes had seen it. And behold the half was not told me. You exceed in wisdom and prosperity the report which I heard. How blessed are your men, how blessed are these your servants who stand before you continually and hear your wisdom.* (1 Kings 10:6-8) And if it was a marvelous thing to be a servant of the great King Solomon how much more so to be the lowliest slave of the King of kings and Lord of lords!

4. What went wrong? How can we explain evil and death in the world?

Now this is Douglas Adams' second great question, Why do people die? (The third being why do they spend so much of the intervening time wearing digital watches. He is a satirist, we must remember!) In truth we are talking about two questions, that of evil and that of death, that have the same answer for the biblical counselor. Romans 5:12 says: *Therefore, just as through one man sin entered into the world and death through sin and so death spread to all men because all sinned.* Death is a result of sin which came through Adam, but it has been propagated by all his descendants, and now all commit sin, and all are subject to death. It is a result of man's free will and his choice to use that freedom to enter into rebellion.

These questions will be answered quite differently by the worldly wise. For them, death is simply part of the natural order. For the Christian it is anything but natural, even if it is normal. For most of these secular gurus, sin is a myth. Man is, for the most part, naturally good, and it is only his environment that determines otherwise. If he *is* evil, Skinner might argue that he has not been justly compensated. Maslow might say he hasn't had his needs met. Freud might say he was wronged in his deep past. All these approaches propagate a victim mentality. If I am a result of my environment, then my problems are external to myself and therefore insurmountable at least without a change in those external circumstances over which I have no real control. I am relieved of any responsibility, then, for my actions. Unfortunately, relieved of any responsibility, I am also relieved of any power to change my condition, begging the question once again, just what do these secular counselors believe they possibly have to offer?

5. *Where can I find hope?*

Do these secular counselors really *offer* any hope? They themselves are the only hope they have to offer, and it is difficult to see just what hope that may truly be. In fact, it creates an outright slavery to these individuals without ever any real liberation. After all, can any man ever truly solve *my* problems?

To the Christian, Jesus says: *I am the way and the truth and the life; no one comes to the Father but through Me.* (John 14:6) The only begotten Son of God died on the cross of Calvary to effect our redemption. That is our hope. First Corinthians 15:20 says: *But now Christ has been raised from the dead, the first fruits of those who are asleep.* If Jesus is the first fruits then surely all of us who follow Him represent the main harvest. We too hope to rise from the dead.

One might ask just why the crucifixion was necessary. Couldn't God just have wiped away our sins without it? He could not! As we will see in chapter 4, grace has no independent existence apart from the law. Lawless grace might better be termed license! After all, why, then, could one simply not do anything he desires without any consequences ever? That is as foreign to God's character as anything can be, and it creates a world that I would not want to live in. We need to know that our sins do have consequences, and that those consequences ordered the most horrible of deaths for God's only begotten Son. Grace is not extended by erasing consequences but by our God paying them in our place!

6. How can I change and eradicate the evil that is within me?

At first glance this question seems like question 5 in a different form but it is not. Question 5 speaks of redemption and question 6 of sanctification. Question 5 speaks of Jesus Christ and Question 6 of the Holy Spirit. Question 5 asks where do I go and question 6 asks how do I get there. Question 5 is a one-time event in the life of a believer and question 6 is a process that lasts until he leaves this life. Question 5 represents a new beginning but question 6 represents everything that follows from that beginning. Philippians 1:6 says: *For I am confident of this very thing, that He who began a good work in you* (redemption), *will perfect it* (sanctification) *until the day of Christ Jesus.* Further, Romans 8:29a says: *For those whom He foreknew* (redemption), *He also predestined to become conformed to the image of His Son* (sanctification). While Jesus Christ gave us the hope of a new resurrection and escape from death, the Holy Spirit forms us to live that life even though to an imperfect degree even in the here and now. Redemption speaks of freedom from the consequences of sin, and sanctification speaks of freedom from sin itself. We do not realize that completely as long as we remain in the flesh, but we do continually move toward that goal, and with it, we receive the peace and joy in the present of that life which will extend to all eternity.

Of course, human responsibility comes into play here as well. Obviously, sanctification is not entirely just a passive process in which we sit back and watch the Holy Spirit work. Sanctification comes through the passionate exercise of the five pillars of Christian living which I shall develop more fully in the next chapter: the pillars of Bible, prayer, church, service, and offering.

Truly, since in his eyes man is not evil in and of himself, the secular counselor denies the very relevance of this question since it is the environment that must be fixed and nothing truly internal to man. Ah but the Christian counselor knows better!

7. *What is my responsibility toward my fellow man?*

Christ did not come just to heal the relationship between God and Man. In the beginning, Man, out of all Creation, was created in the image of God. It isn't that men were created in God's image but Man was. A multiple-person God created multiple-person Man in His image. Thus, it is mankind as a race that was created in our triune God's image and not any one of us as individuals. That image was tarnished by the fall and it cannot be restored unless the relationships among men are also restored. In the prayer our Lord Jesus Christ uttered on behalf of his disciples on the night in which He was betrayed He said: *I do not ask on behalf of these alone but for those also who believe in Me through their word; that they may all be one; even as You, Father, are in Me and I in You, that they also may be in Us so that the world may believe that You sent Me.* (John 17:20-21) It was His prayer that we, all those who are called by His name, be one, displaying once again the glorious image of God so that the world may believe. The entire theme of Paul's epistle to the Ephesians is summed up in these words in chapter 1 verses 9-10: *He made known to us the mystery of His will according to His kind intention which He purposed in Him with a view to an administration suitable to the fullness of the times that is the summing up of all things in Christ things in the heavens and things on the earth in Him.* This is God's purpose for us as a race, and it begins with the institution of the Church.

Clearly it is our God's will that all his people be unite—truly united—under His banner. Our secular counselors would have no particular guidance in this area except in as much as the counselee's relationships benefited herself.

8. *What is my final destiny and the destiny of the world?*

This particular question is the one in which the church is most poorly nourished today. We are quite clear on *some* kind of celestial destiny for all those who have believed, but little is the topic treated from the pulpit. Pastors do not teach eschatology because they themselves don't understand it and are often afraid of it. Indeed, historical interpretations of the book of Revelation have plagued the church ever since Origen injected the damnable heresy of allegoric interpretation of the Scriptures into the church during the early part of the third century, a doctrinal disease from which the church has never fully recovered. Nevertheless, a thorough understanding of biblical prophecy and the future hope it offers can be absolutely transforming to the Christian nourished by its bounty. If you find yourself in that category of those who do not well understand eschatology, please see my own study of the matter in my work, *The Vultures' End.*

Despite the horribly mal-nourished state of the church today in the area of biblical prophecy, there can be no question that we should find an abundance of hope and knowledge of that future life even in the meanest of Christians compared to anything our secular friends have to offer us. We have the security of life eternal beyond the grave in a perfect place with our loving and all-powerful God where every tear will be forever wiped from our eyes, and where no sickness shall ever more rack our bodies.

The best the secular counselor can do is distract his counselee from the reality of the emptiness of her position in his world. Keep on ignoring the elephant, he says to himself in those rare moments of lucidness. And his counselee continues her blind journey through life, hand in hand with her blind mentor.

Thus, considering all of these eight questions, it is the biblical counselor's task to cure what I call the spiritual nearsightedness of his counselee. The natural men and women of this world are focused on the things of this world and entirely incapable of seeing beyond them. The secular counselor, far from treating this spiritual nearsightedness, has no recourse but to do his best to propagate it and get his counselee's mind off of eternal things. By contrast, the answers to the eight fundamental questions of life which the secular counselor cannot successfully navigate are absolutely central to everything the biblical counselor and the Christian school teacher teach and central to the way they live their own lives. The book of Genesis tells us of the story of Esau who foolishly sold his birthright to fill his belly. Anyone will readily see that Esau acted beyond foolishly, and yet so many, even Christians, are prone to the same kind of mistakes, despising their own birthrights as sons and daughters of the Great King out of desire for the fleeting pleasures of sin or, on the contrary, out of fear for the crushing weight of the world. Yet neither those fleeting pleasures nor that crushing weight are worthy to be compared to the glory that shall be revealed in us. This we believe; this we teach; this we live; and in this hope we die!

Reflection: Think on some of the past ways you have run your classroom that focused on the present and temporary rather than the future eternal. What should you change in light of a more far-sighted view of discipline? If you are working in a group discuss this question together.

III. Spiritual Warfare

Now before digging into the content of this chapter, let me start by saying what I do *not* intend to do here. I do not intend to give a guide as to engaging demonic hosts in the classroom. I will not speak of demon possession nor exorcism nor anything of the like. I shall speak, rather, of the day-to-day trench warfare in which all Christians and to a very real extent all mankind are involved, whether we like it or not. I want to approach this topic from three different angles. First of all, what is the nature of this war? Are we primarily on the offensive or the defensive? Secondly, how do we build the warrior? How can I, as a soldier under the banner of Jesus Christ, prepare for the day of battle? Finally, who is the enemy and what are his battle tactics?

Nature of the War

Are we on the offensive or defensive? It is a very simple question and yet one to which many Christians would respond incorrectly. To determine the answer, let us look at Matthew 16:18 when Jesus, affirming Peter's statement of faith said: *I also say to you that you are Peter, and upon this rock I will build my church, and the gates of Hades will not overpower it.*

Now this verse is not what we might at first imagine it to be. It is difficult to understand because it is a rather complex metaphor. A metaphor is a poetic device often used in the Scriptures to help us visualize an otherwise abstract concept. There are many metaphors in the Scriptures. Most use the verb *to be* to create a grammatical equivalence between the object described and the object used to describe it. One very prominent metaphor is when Jesus said, *I am the light of the world.* Jesus is not a light in a literal sense but visualizing Him as light can help us understand something about who He really claimed to be. Similarly, Jesus said to us: *You are the salt of the earth.* Once again, we are not truly salt; we are simply like salt in some way, and the image helps us understand the proper role that we, as believers, are to exercise here in this world.

Matthew 16:18, however, is a particularly complex metaphor which goes beyond a simple comparison connected with the verb *to be.* Once, in a Bible study with a high school youth group I asked each young person to draw a picture of the image this verse brought to mind. Now with the I-am-the-light-of-the-world verse I would just draw a light bulb or a candle. With the salt of the earth verse I might draw a salt shaker. But what does one draw for Matthew 16:18? All manners of drawings appeared. These young people had no idea how to interpret this metaphor!

To decipher it, we have to understand three different words and the contribution that each one makes. These words are *rock, church,* and *gates.* We will begin with the word *church.*

Just what did the disciples understand by the word *church*? Have you ever considered that in the day Jesus uttered those words the church did not exist, and that this is the very first use of the word in the entire Bible? Why didn't Jesus' disciples stop Him right there and ask Him, *Jesus just what do you mean by* church*? I've never heard that word before!* They certainly would *not* have thought of a church building. Church buildings did not even come into common use until the reign of Constantine at the beginning of the fourth century.

The Greek word εκκλησια *(ekklesia)* translated *church* is a compound formed by the preposition *ek,* meaning *out of,* and the verb *kaleo,* meaning *to call.* The word *ekklesia* means, then, *those who are called out* and is most properly translated *assembly.* Among other uses, it referred to the governmental democratic assembly of Athens consisting of all freeborn male citizens of the city. Matthew 16:18 uses the word in a military context, so it might more properly be seen as an army of the elect.

The second word we need to understand is the word *rock.* Before we dig into the contribution of this word to the metaphor, we must clarify *who* it refers to. It absolutely does not refer to the apostle Peter, as has been so steadfastly claimed by the Catholic Church. Peter, which means *rock,* is better thought of as a small rock and the word translated *rock* carries more the meaning of a huge boulder. This can refer to no one other than Jesus himself. Peter is the little stone that bears some resemblance to the big one but Jesus is the rock over which He would found His Church. This usage recalls to mind Nebuchadnezzar's dream in Daniel 2 in which a huge statue representing a succession of Gentile kingdoms is smashed by a rock that becomes a great mountain filling the entire earth. There is no question that Nebuchadnezzar's rock also referred to Jesus.

Now as to the metaphor, after having received an invitation from the fierce Yali tribe only months after they had killed two other missionaries, Don Richardson, in his book *Lords of the Earth,* describes his approach with two companions to the unevangelized village. Gazing at their destination in the distance, they groaned as their native guides chose the path that led down into the valley from where they would have to climb up again to the village from below. They were exhausted, and it would have been far easier just to follow the ridge and descend directly to the village from above. They complained but the guides insisted. Why? *It is bad etiquette to approach a Yali village from above* they were told. *That is what enemies do to give themselves a military advantage. To show good will and peaceful intention you must take the trouble to climb up to the village from below placing yourself at a disadvantage.* The rock of Matthew 16:18 represents the high ground which gives an army a military advantage over its enemy.

However, *rock* does mean a bit more than that at the same time. Having taken so much trouble a moment ago to refute the idea that the word translated *church* refers to a building, I must now admit that in a metaphorical sense—sort of a metaphor within a metaphor— it *does* represent a building. The fact that it is *built* rather than assembled gives it this sense. One must wonder if Peter was remembering Jesus' words to him when he wrote the following:

> **And coming to Him as to a living stone which has been rejected by men but is choice and precious in the sight of God, [5] you also, as living stones, are being built up as a spiritual house for a holy priesthood to offer up spiritual sacrifices acceptable to God through Jesus Christ. [6] For this is contained in Scripture: "BEHOLD I LAY IN ZION A CHOICE STONE, A PRECIOUS CORNER stone, AND HE WHO BELIEVES IN HIM WILL NOT BE DISAPPOINTED." [7] This precious value, then, is for you who believe; but for those who disbelieve, "THE STONE WHICH THE BUILDERS REJECTED, THIS BECAME THE**

VERY CORNER stone," [8] and "A STONE OF STUMBLING AND A ROCK OF OFFENSE"; for they stumble because they are disobedient to the word, and to this doom they were also appointed. (1 Peter 2:4-8)

It also brings to mind Jesus' own words in the sermon on the Mount.

"Therefore, everyone who hears these words of Mine and acts on them may be compared to a wise man who built his house on the rock. [25] And the rain fell, and the floods came, and the winds blew, and slammed against that house; and yet it did not fall, for it had been founded on the rock. (Matthew 7:24-25)

It is true that Peter uses the word, $\lambda\iota\theta\sigma\sigma$ *(lithos)*, here instead of $\pi\varepsilon\tau\rho\alpha$ *(petra)*, but it has a similar meaning. Here we see that Jesus is the foundational stone or even rock as we find in the Sermon on the Mount. Peter was another living stone built on top of that living cornerstone that is Jesus Christ. All together, we are built into a spiritual house, a living, breathing temple of the Living God for a royal priesthood which shall stand even as it dismantles the gates of hell. This brings to mind Revelation 3:12:

The one who overcomes, I will make him a pillar in the temple of My God, and he will not go out from it anymore; and I will write on him the name of My God and the name of the city of My God, the new Jerusalem which comes down out of heaven from My God, and My new name.

We also recall 1 Corinthians 3 where Paul describes the building of a temple over the foundation which is Jesus Christ with good works composed of gold, silver, and precious stones. However, in the end he concludes that the temple is built of believers themselves in verses 16-17:

[16] Do you not know that you are a temple of God and *that* the Spirit of God dwells in you? [17] If anyone destroys the temple of God, God will destroy that person; for the temple of God is holy, and that is what you are.

Thus the *ekklesia* of Christ is literally a conquering army, but metaphorically a grand temple in which the Spirit of God dwells which promises refuge to all who would come to it.

Finally, we come to the word *gates*. This implies a fortified city with walls all around it. The gates represented a city's military weak point toward which invading armies would focus their attacks. If the gate could be breached, the city's defenders would lose the advantage of their walls and would have little chance against the massive attacking army. Hollywood has reproduced the scene of the military battering of the city gates in film after film from *Lord of the Rings* to *Braveheart*. The question that remains is, who is behind those walls and who is battering down the gates? Is the Church behind those walls? The city is Hades. That is not where the Church lives! The Church is, then, the attacking army battering down the gates!

That the Christian is on the offensive is confirmed in Paul's description of the armor of God in Ephesians 6. The one offensive weapon Paul gives to the Christian soldier is *the sword of the Spirit* whereas the passage speaks of *the flaming arrows* of the evil one. A sword is made for fighting face to face, close in and personal. It is a weapon of attack. On the contrary the flaming arrows of the evil one conjure up an image of a defending army hiding behind its stone wall trying desperately to weaken and discourage the attackers.

Thus, we see that contrary to all our modern thinking, it is not Hades that is on the offensive; it is the Church! How often have we spoken of Satan's attacks! Satan does not attack. Satan only counter attacks those who are a danger to him. Have you ever heard the line, *Satan doesn't attack non-Christians because he already has them*? The erroneous implication of this statement is that he has the capability of winning those he doesn't *already have*. Let me be clear! Not one person that Satan has lost can he ever hope to regain. The only real question is exactly how many he will lose and his battle strategy is designed to minimize his losses because he knows that to gain ground is beyond his capacity.

So why exactly is the Church on the offensive? What do we hope to gain? Myriads are the human souls held behind the fortified walls of that great city of Hades. We fight to set the captives free! It is for our unsaved brothers, sisters, mothers, fathers, sons, daughters, friends, neighbors, and yes students and their parents, that we fight. And the gates of Hades shall not prevail against us!

Formation of the Soldier

Since Christian teachers are certainly front-line soldiers of Jesus Christ, it is imperative that we begin acting like it. Soldiering is a full-time job and that does not mean for forty hours a week. We may spend less than forty hours with our students, but even when we are not with them, we continue our preparation for the next day, building towers, ladders, and rams to breach the walls of the city and constantly disciplining our own spiritual bodies and sharpening our skills to withstand in the day of battle. As Paul says in 1 Corinthians 9:27: *but I discipline my body and make it my slave so that after I have preached to others, I myself will not be disqualified.* Being a Christian soldier is a 24-hour-a-day 365-day-a-year job. A Christian school teacher who is not mindful of this reality cannot be effective in achieving this high objective of evangelizing and discipling the children in her charge.

Just how then do I do this? What does it mean to discipline one's body? What are the basic elements of the Christian life? How does a Christian occupy his time? Note I am not speaking of doctrine here; I am speaking of practice. Just how does a Christian act? What does he do? A Christian, in order to be complete, must learn to exercise and thrive in five areas which I call the five pillars of Christian living. These pillars are Bible, prayer, church, service, and offering. If we excel in these areas, we are truly well-formed soldiers of Christ. Let us consider these pillars one by one.

1. Bible

The Bible is, in the entirety of its sixty-six books, the inspired Word of God. It is His complete and sufficient revelation to mankind that provides everything man needs to live a righteous life in this world.

The first four verses of Psalm 1 say the following:

> **How blessed is the man who does not walk in the counsel of the wicked, Nor stand in the path of sinners, Nor sit in the seat of scoffers!** **² But his delight is in the law of the LORD, And in His law he meditates day and night. ³ He will be like a tree firmly planted by streams of water, Which yields**

its fruit in its season. And its leaf does not wither; And in whatever he does, he prospers. [4] The wicked are not so But they are like chaff which the wind drives away.

Now the first three verses speak of the righteous man. Verse one tells us what he doesn't do, namely, walk in the counsel of the wicked, stand in the path of sinners, nor sit in the seat of scoffers! How does he have the strength to avoid all these things? Verse two speaks loudly and clearly. *His delight is in the law of the Lord, and in His law he meditates day and night.* The righteous man is firmly rooted in the Word of God. It is his joy to study and meditate on it. Verse three makes a comparison between this righteous man and a tree planted by streams of water. The stream is the Word of God that nourishes us and makes us strong. A strongly rooted tree is absolutely immovable, absent the most extreme circumstances. Finally, verse 4 contrasts this righteous man with the wicked who is blown like chaff in the wind at the time of threshing by every latest fad and culture change. Now let me ask you, oh Christian soldier, do you resemble more that tree or the chaff blown away by the wind? Are you uncertain of your ways? Are you inconstant, wandering like a butterfly from one beautiful flower to another? Are you sometimes uncertain as to what is right and what is wrong, or are you firm and unwavering? Do you suffer, as we spoke in the previous chapter, from a problem of spiritual near-sightedness, or do you see clearly that which the eyes cannot perceive?

Now we are not speaking of a simple Bible reading each morning, much less a devotional book. We studied in the last chapter the sufficiency and the power of the Word. Do you let it mold you? How do you study? Do you merely read through? Surely this is not a bad thing. In fact, I would recommend any new Christian to read the Bible straight through and do it three of four times. Still the day comes when reading the Bible through falls into a pattern of diminishing returns as I start remembering more and more of the Scripture I have read before and assimilating less and less new things. In that day, every believer must become a miner to continue to extract the riches of God's Word. This takes purpose and effort.

Many books have been written about techniques for studying the Bible, and I certainly have no intention that this volume should be turned to that purpose. Personally, these books have contributed little to my own study. Nevertheless, I would like to provide some basic suggestions as to how to mine those nuggets of truth from the Word that shall never come from a casual reading.

Outside the Bible itself, there are two absolute essentials to good Bible study for which there are no substitutes: a good journaling tool of which a computer is far superior to a pen and notebook, and access to multiple biblical commentaries. Personally, I like the *Ultimate Bible Commentary* I have on my Kindle which features the classical commentators Barnes, Henry, Clarke, Calvin, Wesley, and Spurgeon. That way, I can compare each of these to my study Bible footnotes and other commentaries to which I may have access, to see which might bring me insight on a particular question or passage.

In studying a book, it is good to start out with a goal if it is simply to understand the content better. Some books, like Genesis, are easy to read and easy to wrap the mind around. Others, such as Isaiah or Psalms, take considerably more effort. The first thing I do in any Bible study is read through the book and take copious notes. After that, sometimes I may take days at a time without even opening my Bible but just studying my notes. I may categorize them thematically and place what may be distant passages in the context of the Bible together. This often brings about significant revelations. I also try to write down as many questions as I can generate and then search for the answers in my commentaries.

Another technique is to do word studies. When you notice that a particular author likes a particular word, underline every use of it in the text. Count the times he uses it and note how. A working knowledge of the biblical languages is also useful. One doesn't have to be fluent but it is helpful to be able to navigate a lexicon and an interlinear text and understand the uses of a particular word in the original language. Making outlines of a book or a text is also helpful. I also sometimes examine the chronology of a given book. This is easy for some books, such as Ezekiel, which often provides specific dates for its prophesies. On the other hand, the book of Jeremiah is quite a challenge as it is obviously written entirely out of chronological order. I have also attempted to study the gospels chronologically which is difficult since we often see a different order of events between Matthew and Luke. I have even gone back and tried to count the number of years through Genesis, the books of Judges and the Kings in order to determine a date for the Creation.

Finally, there is no substitute for teaching, and if you can't teach, trying to write a summary of what you have learned is wonderful.

Certainly there are a wide variety of ways to study the Bible and employing these techniques to the Word of God can supply a lifetime of marvelous experiences in the Word that simple read-throughs can never effect. It is the obligation of the soldier of Christ to continually return to his source of strength. After all, if we gird ourselves with the belt of truth, truth is found in the Scriptures. If our breastplate is of righteousness, righteousness comes, as Psalm 1 instructs us, from a constant meditation on the laws of God found in the Scriptures. If our feet are shod with the gospel of peace, where is it that we learn the gospel? If our shield is of faith, faith comes by hearing which comes by the Word of Christ (Romans 10:17). That particular passage was written back when a person's only access to the Word of God was the pubic readings held in their synagogues and house churches. Today, with multiple Bibles in each household, we can skip the hearing step and go directly to the Word ourselves. If our helmet is of our salvation, where do we learn of this great salvation? Finally, we are told that even our sword of the Spirit is the Word of God.

Truly, without the Word of God, there is no soldier at all, and a true soldier immerses himself daily in it, training himself constantly to wield this supreme weapon of our spiritual war.

2. Prayer

Paul finishes that great passage in Ephesians 6 delineating the armor of God with the following addendum in verse 18: *With all prayer and petition, pray at all times in the Spirit, and with this in view, be on the alert with all perseverance and petition for all the saints.* Prayer is the second great pillar of the faith, and I am really convinced it is something that few Christians do well.

In 1 Thessalonians 5:17 we are instructed to pray without ceasing. Just what does that look like? Obviously it doesn't mean to spend our lives with our heads bowed and our eyes closed. It does mean, however, that we should remain in a continual attitude of prayer and should set apart frequent significant blocks of time for it. Truthfully, I believe that as a Christian practically from birth up to my

55 years of age, I have only in the last few years begun to understand how to pray. Normally our prayers are far too superficial and far too frugal. Prayer is something that should happen both individually and in groups and in both formats, time should be ample and prayer unrestricted. In group prayer, I have been frustrated by the amount of time lost in sharing superficial prayer requests, and then, when we actually get around to praying, by feeling bound to the long list we have thus generated. How refreshing it has been to gather with a small group of men with the unrestricted time it requires to really pour out our hearts to God and the freedom to be led by the Spirit! Another good, dynamic way to pray in larger groups is what has been called popcorn prayer where every individual agrees to pray very short, one-or-two-sentence prayers as to whatever is on his heart and then pass to someone else. Thus, everyone gets multiple opportunities to pray.

Enough on the techniques! What are the elements of prayer? There are five that we should consider: praise, thanksgiving, repentance, intersession, and petition. It is so easy to jump straight to petitions, which is why I personally believe that order is important. Whenever I dedicate time to prayer, I try to begin with the other aspects before turning to the requests that are closest to my heart. Let us examine each of these five elements of prayer individually.

Praise is a good way to start off. The second element of prayer is thanksgiving, and it might be easy at times to confuse the two. Praise is simply lauding God for who He is and for the mighty things He has done. It focuses on His attributes. I personally am an astronomy enthusiast and contemplating the galaxies full of suns and planets beyond our capacity to count at distances beyond our capacity to imagine reminds me of the hugeness of our God and serves as a medium for my praise to Him. The prayer that Jesus taught his disciples begins with praise, *Our Father who is in heaven hallowed be Your name.* (Matthew 6:9) Addressing the Lord as *our Father who is in heaven* and then declaring His name *hallowed* are items of praise. Meditating on many of the Psalms that emphasize praise may also help us in this area.

Meanwhile, thanksgiving focusses on the *specific* blessings of life like a scholarship to a good college, the promotion we got at work, the life partner God has given us, a faithful friend, the provision and joy of a wonderful home-cooked meal, a warm smile, a funny joke— and even disagreeable things! First Thessalonians 5:18 tells us: *in everything give thanks; for this is God's will for you in Christ Jesus.* I cannot read this verse without thinking of the story told by Corrie Ten Boom in *The Hiding Place.* When she and her sister Betsy first arrived at the Nazi concentration camp during World War II, they managed to sneak a small Bible past the guards and into their barracks. They had just read and shared that verse together and had decided it was time to put the words into practice. Corrie thanked God that they had managed to smuggle the Bible in undetected. She thanked God for the company of her sister in that awful place. She even thanked God for the tightly packed bunks in the barracks because it would give them opportunity to share Jesus with more people. Then her sister turned to the question of the fleas in their beds. At that Corrie balked, *Betsy I'm not going to thank God for the fleas!* Gently Betsy reminded her of the verse they had just read, and she grudgingly capitulated. In the days that followed, Corrie and Betsy found tremendous freedom within their barracks to witness for Jesus Christ to their fellow prisoners. Of themes they would have been quickly punished for at any other time during the day, they could freely speak in the evenings. One day Betsy overheard two guards talking, one ordering the other to go into the barracks to remove a sick woman. The other guard refused saying, *I'm not going in there! That place is full of fleas!* Their freedom to share the gospel in the barracks was because of the fleas! Betsy waited triumphantly to share with Corrie the news that many women had come to know Christ because of the fleas. I'm sure that evening Corrie thanked God for the fleas once again, but this time with a very different heart.

And this has been my experience as well. Within the most difficult periods of my life, God has spoken to me in very special ways. I can always thank Him for being in control and for making me pass through trials I would never choose for myself because in the end, He knows what is best for me, and He has a purpose in every single one. Truly we are told that *all things work together for the good to those who love God and are called according to His purpose.* (Romans 8:28) And I am guaranteed that *the sufferings of this present time are not worthy to be compared with the glory that is to be revealed to us.* (Romans 8:18) Thus, although we may not see it, fleas are just as much a part of God's blessing as a home-cooked meal, and it behooves us to give thanks as much for those things that give us sorrow as for those that give us joy.

The third item of the five aspects of prayer is repentance. First John 1:9 assures us that: *If we confess our sins, He is faithful and righteous to forgive us our sins and to cleanse us from all unrighteousness.* This repentance is more than simply acknowledging my specific shortcomings; it is constantly examining my own heart and praying the Lord to reveal my sins. Then I agree with God in prayer that my sin is sin, and I plead with Him to strengthen me to overcome it and to transform my life. However, repentance is not always individual. We should also engage in corporal repentance. Many of the giants of the Bible such as Nehemiah and Daniel and many of the prophets cried out to the Lord for the sin of their nation, sin that they were quite likely not even complicit in. This also pleases the Lord when we stand in the gap for our fellow man, for our families, for our churches, for our nation, taking the responsibility for their sin upon ourselves and pleading God's forgiveness.

The fourth item is intersession and while technically, prayers for our children or our parents or for our closest friends might truly be acts of intersession, they are also often yearnings which are very close to our own hearts. When interceding, we should work from the outside in remembering those people and events who do not emotionally stir us before we pray for those that do. We should intercede for institutions, for the Church and our individual congregations by name and for our governing authorities as we are commanded in 1 Timothy 2:1-2. We should also remember those Christians across the world who are suffering persecution and those with the opposite challenge of prosperity and comfort which can so weaken our spiritual muscles.

Finally, the last item on the list is that one we would like to put first petition. We know how to ask for things, but we don't always know very well the things we ought to ask for. How often we pray with that spiritual nearsightedness, thinking of our physical wants and needs and neglecting the far more important spiritual needs! This rule applies not only to our petitions for ourselves, but for those for whom we intercede. It is quite interesting that in writing the book of Ephesians from a Roman house arrest, Paul did not ask for prayers that he be released, but for courage to speak boldly as he ought, prayers to strengthen him to be an effective witness for Christ. (Ephesians 6:18-20) These are the kinds of things that we also ought to pray for ourselves and for those around us. We should pray that

God would focus our thoughts in our Bible studies, giving us new insights. We should pray for wisdom to handle the situations of life, more than pray that those situations might go away.

3. Church

One of the gravest and subtlest heresies in the church today is what I might call the Footprints Phenomenon. All have heard that beautiful anonymous poem of two sets of footprints in the sand of life that represent the believer and Jesus Christ walking side by side. All of us have sighed in contentment at the conclusion of the poem when the author asks why he sees only one set of footprints in all the most difficult moments and discovers that, rather than being abandoned by Christ, he was being carried through those times. My question is just why was this individual walking through life all alone in the first place? This poem is a glaring example of what is perhaps one of the subtlest and most venomous brands of bad theology in the Church today! It is the exaltation of the personal relationship with Jesus Christ that fosters the idea that we can do Christianity alone! Now there is hardly a dedicated Christian from whose mouth the phrase *personal relationship with Jesus Christ* has not flowed on numerous occasions, particularly during encounters of personal evangelism. However, this phrase is entirely unbiblical. Nowhere in the New Testament is anyone called to a personal relationship with Jesus Christ. We are called individually to a very corporate relationship with Jesus Christ. To be sure there *is* a personal aspect to that relationship, but the root nature of our calling is to enter into a corporate covenant with Jesus Christ to be part of His body. And that body is named the Church.

The corporate nature of our calling is attested to throughout Scriptures beginning with the very first use of the word church in Matthew 16:18: *I also say to you that you are Peter and upon this rock I will build My church; and the gates of Hades will not overpower it,* and continuing with another scripture we have quoted before, John 17:20-21 Jesus prayer for his disciples and for us just before He was arrested: *I do not ask on behalf of these alone but for those also who believe in Me through their word; that they may all be one; even as You, Father, are in Me and I in You, that they also may be in Us so that the world may believe that You sent Me.* Here we see once again that the fulfillment of our commission to evangelize the world depends on our commitment to that body. The theme of the entire book of Ephesians is summed up in verses 1:9-10: *He made known to us the mystery of His will according to His kind intention which He purposed in Him with a view to an administration suitable to the fullness of the times, that is, the summing up of all things in Christ, things in the heavens and things on the earth.* The rest of the book deals with that theme of the summing up of all things in Christ speaking of the union of Jew and Gentile in one body and how that unity is applied in all our human relationships within that body.

Our commitment to the Church must be unwavering, and that commitment calls us to a relationship with a local congregation. It simply is not enough to attend church every Sunday. The purpose of church is not just to teach us how to live out our individual personal relationships with Christ; its purpose is to bind us together as one body, as one brotherhood to the glory of our Father and our Lord Jesus Christ and as a testimony to those outside. It is a place, then, where we should strive to develop our primary relationships in life outside our blood family, a place where we go to *serve* much more than to be served. This is the commitment every Christian should have to the Body of Christ and above all, the Christian school teacher. Otherwise, how can that teacher hope to be an effective soldier in freeing the captives? Truth be told, the lack of a healthy church body relegates the strongest evangelist to ineffectiveness.

4. Offering

Whatever the weaknesses we might speak of concerning the first three pillars, they are quite often preached in the church. These last two are far more neglected, and yet these actually speak of putting our Christianity into practice. A man or woman of God knows that in this life nothing that we possess truly belongs to us. As the servants in the Parable of the Talents, we are only *stewards* of everything in our possession. We cannot consider that only ten percent belongs to God when truly He is Lord of the whole. As Christians and children of the King, we are called to be generous administrators of our Father's resources.

We should give cheerfully. Second Corinthians 9:6-7 says: *Now this I say, he who sows sparingly will also reap sparingly, and he who sows bountifully will also reap bountifully. Each one must do just as he has purposed in his heart, not grudgingly or under compulsion, for God loves a cheerful giver.* Thus we see that giving is a test and a measure of our faith. What does our level of giving then say about our level of faith? Even in the book of Malachi 3:10 the Father exhorts us: *Bring the whole tithe into the storehouse so that there may be food in My house, and test Me now in this," says the* LORD *of hosts, "if I will not open for you the windows of heaven and pour out for you a blessing until it overflows.* Even King Solomon in the book of Proverbs verse 11:24 observes: *There is one who scatters and yet increases all the more And there is one who withholds what is justly due and yet it results only in want.*

Further, giving is an act not only of faith, but also of worship. In the book of Malachi, the prophet rebukes the people for giving to God unworthily. In verses 1:6-8 he says:

> **'A son honors his father and a servant his master. Then if I am a father, where is My honor? And if I am a master, where is My respect?' says the** LORD **of hosts to you O priests who despise My name. But you say, 'How have we despised Your name?' [7] You are presenting defiled food upon My altar. But you say, 'How have we defiled You?' In that you say, 'The table of the** LORD **is to be despised.' [8] But when you present the blind for sacrifice, is it not evil? And when you present the lame and sick, is it not evil? Why not offer it to your governor? Would he be pleased with you? Or would he receive you kindly?" says the** LORD **of hosts.**

We give to the Lord, not because He needs our gifts, but because He is the King, and one does not worship a king with an unworthy gift! Verse 14 says: *for I am a great King," says the* LORD *of hosts, "and My name is feared among the nations.* Our offerings to the Lord must be worthy of a king. Shall we give a gift that cost us little? When we toss our spare change into the offering plate, is this a gift that honors our King? From the human worldly perspective of the church, we may consider that every little bit counts, but it is clear how God looks at this from a heavenly perspective. However, we must note that our King is different from earthly kings because the poor are capable of pleasing Him even more, at times, than the rich. This Jesus made clear as He affirmed the widows' two mites above all the much larger gifts of the wealthy in Luke 21. And Jesus can and will do extraordinary things with even a little, given in true faith. Oh that I might have known the extraordinary little boy who brought his lunch to Jesus in John 6 while his rather embarrassed Uncle Andrew looked on. He was just naïve enough to believe that Jesus would value his gift and use it for His glory, lacking the worldly understanding of his patron disciple. Indeed, Jesus gave bread and fish to five thousand families that day, and the next day they were dissatisfied and sought more, but one little boy gave bread and fish to *Jesus*. How much wiser was that boy than all the disciples, and how much even more so than the fickle crowds! Dear Jesus give us the faith of that widow and that young boy to give without reservation as You lead!

5. Service

But it is not enough to give of our treasures, albeit generously; we must also give of ourselves. At the beginning of his great discourse on giving in 2 Corinthians, Paul describes the example of the Macedonians, in all likelihood led by the extraordinary Philippians:

> **In a great ordeal of affliction, their abundance of joy and their deep poverty overflowed in the wealth of their liberality. [3] For I testify that according to their ability and beyond their ability, they gave of their own accord, [4] begging us with much urging for the favor of participation in the support of the saints, [5] and this not as we had expected, but they first gave themselves to the Lord and to us by the will of God. (8:2-5)**

What an extraordinary attitude among these poor Christians of giving, not only of their scarce resources, but also of their very selves! Truly the Lord exhorts us in Matthew 9:35 *If anyone wants to be first, he shall be last of all and servant of all.* Paul adds to this using the example of Jesus when he says in Philippians 2:5-7: *Have this attitude in yourselves which was also in Christ Jesus, who, although He existed in the form of God did not regard equality with God a thing to be grasped, but emptied Himself, taking the form of a bond-servant and being made in the likeness of men.* Indeed, Jesus Himself, after He had washed His disciples' feet, said: *If I, then, the Lord and the Teacher, washed your feet, you also ought to wash one another's feet. For I gave you an example that you also should do as I did to you. Truly, truly I say to you, a slave is not greater than his master, nor is one who is sent greater than the one who sent him. If you know these things you are blessed if you do them.* (John 13:14-17)

Now these verses only set the standard, but they give us little practical advice as to how to carry it out. Many passages could be cited here but perhaps the most descriptive is the Parable of the Sheep and the Goats in Matthew 25. Jesus said to the sheep: *Come, you who are blessed of My Father, inherit the kingdom prepared for you from the foundation of the world. For I was hungry, and you gave Me something to eat; I was thirsty, and you gave Me something to drink; I was a stranger, and you invited Me in; naked, and you clothed Me; I was sick, and you visited Me; I was in prison, and you came to Me.* (verses 34-36) Now I would like to point out that the sheep and the goats were not separated by their works; they were separated by species. The Lord first placed all the sheep on one side and the goats on the other. Then He observed that the sheep had similar patterns of service to their fellows, and the goats did not. In other words, their service did not make them sheep; their identity as sheep made them serve. It was simply in their nature to do so.

Now certainly there are many, many ways in this world to serve, but I would like to highlight two. I have great admiration for those couples who have opened up their homes to receive disadvantaged children. The Bible says beautiful things about children and about those who reach out to care for them. In Matthew 18:10 we read: *their angels in heaven continually see the face of My Father who is in heaven.* Earlier in that same chapter in verse 5 the Lord tells us: *whoever receives one such child in My name, receives Me.* Further, James tells us in the last verse of chapter 1: *Pure and undefiled religion in the sight of our God and Father is this: to visit orphans and widows in their distress and to keep oneself unstained by the world.*

Second, I would like to highlight the gift of hospitality. Hospitality was practiced lavishly in the Bible, and anything we call hospitality today is only a dim reflection of the ancient practice. We see it in the examples of the patriarchs who, time after time, opened up their homes to perfect strangers to help them on their way as did both Abraham and Lot for the strangers who turned out to be angels come to destroy Sodom and Gomorra. Lot was even willing to give his own daughters to placate the mob seeking to force themselves onto the men that were under his protection. I do not mean to justify Lot's actions, but it does show the strength of the culture of hospitality in his day. We see it in many other instances such as in that rather horrible story of the Levite and his concubine who stopped overnight in that city in Benjamin in the closing chapters of the book of Judges. We also see it in the woman who provided a place for the prophet Elisha to stay whenever he passed through. In the New Testament, Mary and Martha provided regular hospitality for Jesus when he went to Jerusalem. The early church itself met in the homes of the brethren, and they themselves had an attitude of hospitality that was nearly unsurpassable as is described in these closing verses of Acts 2:

> **And all those who had believed were together and had all things in common; and they began selling their property and possessions and were sharing them with all as anyone might have need. [45] Day by day continuing with one mind in the temple and breaking bread from house to house, they were taking their meals together with gladness and sincerity of heart, praising God and having favor with all the people. [46] And the Lord was adding to their number day by day those who were being saved.**

And also at the end of chapter 4:

> **And the congregation of those who believed were of one heart and soul; and not one of them claimed that anything belonging to him was his own, but all things were common property to them. [33] And with great power, the apostles were giving testimony to the resurrection of the Lord Jesus and abundant grace was upon them all. [34] For there was not a needy person among them, for all who were owners of land or houses would sell them and bring the proceeds of the sales [35] and lay them at the apostles' feet, and they would be distributed to each as any had need.**

Thus, we see the hospitality of those within the church, but Jesus also exhorts us in Luke 14:12-14:

When you give a luncheon or a dinner, do not invite your friends or your brothers or your relatives or rich neighbors, otherwise they may also invite you in return and that will be your repayment. [13] But when you give a reception, invite the poor, the crippled, the lame, the blind, and you will be blessed since they do not have the means to repay you; [14] for you will be repaid at the resurrection of the righteous.

And What about Evangelism?

There may be those who say that I have left out a very critical sixth plank of Christian living, namely that of evangelism. After all was this not the heart of the Great Commission that serves as the very cornerstone and reason for being of the Church today? Jesus said at the end of Matthew's gospel: *Go therefore and make disciples of all the nations, baptizing them in the name of the Father and the Son and the Holy Spirit, teaching them to observe all that I commanded you,* and at the beginning of Acts: *You will receive power when the Holy Spirit has come upon you; and you shall be My witnesses both in Jerusalem and in all Judea and Samaria and even to the remotest part of the earth.*

Let me assure you, this omission has been purposeful. Saint Francis of Assisi once said: *Preach the gospel at all times. When necessary use words.* This statement was indeed the motto of the saint's life! He founded an order dedicated to Christian service as a means of evangelism. And this concept was reflected at times even within the life of Jesus. One very effective day of evangelism, He won the notorious tax collector Zacchaeus without ever opening His mouth more than to say *Come down from that tree. I want to spend some time with you.* And while Peter does tell us in 1 Peter 1:15: *but sanctify Christ as Lord in your hearts, always being ready to make a defense to everyone who asks you to give an account for the hope that is in you, yet with gentleness and reverence.* Truth be told, passages that command the preaching of the gospel to others are extremely few and far between outside these statements of the Great Commission. Even this verse in 1 Peter is decidedly passive. It doesn't tell us to preach, but to be ready to *make an account.* Be ready, that is, when someone notices and asks just as Paul himself experienced in Acts 16:30 when the Philippian jailor fell at his prisoners' feet and asked them: *Sirs, what must I do to be saved?* Now with that kind of head start, evangelism hardly requires any fancy rhetorical skills. Paul and Silas's lives, singing praises through the night and then not escaping when the opportunity was afforded them, spoke much more loudly than any mere words could ever have done. We look back once again at that now thrice cited passage from Jesus' prayer in John 17: *I do not ask on behalf of these alone, but for those also who believe in Me through their word; that they may all be one; even as You, Father, are in Me and I in You, that they also may be in Us so that the world may believe that You sent Me.* The world believing is not a result of eloquent preaching, but of the unity it sees in the Church.

My friends I am strongly convinced that that is exactly how it is. If the church stopped talking so much about preaching the gospel and starting talking a lot more about living the gospel, we would find far more of the sons and daughters of Adam drawn to the Lord. When God's people, founded and grounded in His Word and dedicated one to another and to a life of prayer without ceasing, act out that faith with boundless giving of our treasures and of our very selves, the world must take notice. And how can it be that many will not fall down at our feet as that Philippian jailor did at Paul's and ask us the way of salvation? We let our light so shine before men that they may see our good works and respond by glorifying our Father which is in heaven. (Matthew 5:16) That is how the Great Commission shall be fulfilled. That is how it works! Now to be sure there is an aspect of *go* to it. We cannot all stay at home and hope that the gospel reaches the ends of the earth by itself. However, *preaching* the gospel is of miniscule importance in fulfilling the Commission as compared to *living* it, and this is the task that we as Christian educators must set our hearts to achieve before the young minds and hearts that sit before us day after day.

Knowing the Enemy

Finally, let us turn our attention to the enemy! Just who is it? Is our enemy our own government or foreign governments? Is our enemy one political party or the other? Is our enemy the rich and powerful or the poor and lawless? Is our enemy those priests of other religions?

None of the above! Paul tells us very clearly in Ephesians 6:12: *For our struggle is not against flesh and blood, but against the rulers, against the power,s against the world forces of this darkness, against the spiritual forces of wickedness in the heavenly places.* In short our enemy is the devil and his angels. Now 1 Peter 5:8 says: *Your adversary, the devil, prowls around like a roaring lion, seeking someone to devour.* When a lion shadows a herd of buffalo which animals become his prey? The weak and the sickly particularly the young and even more particularly the young whose mothers are not nearby to protect them! In short *this* lion's most likely victims are the very at-risk children that we serve in our schools.

Now Satan has two primary weapons at his disposal whereby he destroys and devours. First, he is a liar and a deceiver. Our Lord said of Satan in John 8:44: *He was a murderer from the beginning and does not stand in the truth because there is no truth in him. Whenever he speaks a lie he speaks from his own nature, for he is a liar and the father of lies.* Second, he is an accuser and a slanderer. Revelation 12:10, speaking of that future day when all is near completion, says: *the accuser of our brethren has been thrown down, he who accuses them before our God day and night.* Now Satan appears in personal form in the Bible on four occasions outside the book of Revelation. He appears in Genesis 3 lying and deceiving Eve. He appears in Job 1-2 accusing Job before God. He appears in Zechariah 3 accusing Joshua the high priest before God. Then he appears in Matthew 4 and Luke 4, lying and attempting to deceive Jesus Christ. In the book of Revelation, he is called *the accuser of our brethren* in the verse we just cited, but in Revelation 20 at the start of the millennium, Satan is bound and thrown into the abyss *so that he would not deceive the nations any longer until the thousand years were completed.* (verse 3) Then at the end of the Millennium he is released *and will come out to deceive the nations which are in the four corners of the earth.* (verse 8) Finally, in verse 10, it is said of him: *And the devil who deceived them was thrown into the lake of fire and brimstone.* Thus we see from start to finish that Satan alternately lies and accuses, lies and accuses. He lies until he deceives us and causes us to fall into sin. Then he accuses us before God and the rest of the world to effect our condemnation. And he accuses us to our own face to shame us for the very sin he seduced us to commit in the first place.

Satan tells many lies but nearly all of them are simply different forms of three basic lies whose object is to subvert the two basic truths of the gospel as asserted in Hebrews 11:6: *And without faith it is impossible to please Him, for he who comes to God must believe that He is and that He is a rewarder of those who seek Him.* So, in order to please God, we have to believe that *He is* or that He exists and that *He is a rewarder of those who seek Him.* Those are the two basic truths that compose saving faith.

The first great lie of Satan is to subvert that first truth. God does not exist, or if He does not as the Bible describes Him. Perhaps the true God is really the monolithic, vengeful God of Islam. Perhaps he's the deist God who set everything in motion and then left it alone, a distant, impersonal God who doesn't really care. Whatever we believe about God is perfectly fine as long as it's not the truth. Satan may manage to convince us to reject God's reality because otherwise we may have to give up our pet sin. Or on the contrary He may persuade us that a good God wouldn't allow the evil we see in the world. Of course this is a spiritually near-sighted belief that Satan propagates easily. It is indeed difficult to reconcile the reality of all the evil we see with a good God that we don't see. We can only do it if we learn to see this world as only a small part of something vastly bigger to which the suffering of this present time cannot compare. Although we do not understand, we are encouraged forward by Isaiah 40:31: *Yet those who wait for the LORD, Will gain new strength; They will mount up with wings like eagles; They will run and not get tired. They will walk and not become weary.* This is because the evil we see in this world now is only an infinitesimal part of a perfect and glorious eternity. With our eyes of flesh, we are unable to see or imagine anything beyond our own brief lifetimes, and many are just not willing to wait upon the Lord long enough because they have not learned to see with spiritual eyes. Apparently they never look up at the stars. A little earlier in the same chapter of Isaiah, we are told: *Lift up your eyes on high And see who has created these stars, The One who leads forth their host by number; He calls them all by name; Because of the greatness of His might and the strength of His power, Not one of them is missing.* The vastness of the heavens which we can see today better than ever in history with all our modern-day technology speaks to us of the vast God who created them in profound and sublime ways. How could anyone look up at the stars and deny the existence of God?

Satan's second big lie is that God is not good. This is the one he cooed at Eve in the Garden. There was no way for Satan to convince her that God didn't exist. She had walked and talked with Him. But to get her to believe He was holding out on her *was* within his reach. Even Satan's temptation of Jesus was based on trying to make Him forget the goodness of the Father. *Jesus you've been out here for forty days without eating. You don't have the strength to get back to town. If You are going to do the task Your Father gave You You can't let it end this way. Exert your power as His Son to fix this situation because Your Father is not coming through for You.* The other two temptations were also attempts to make Him doubt the plans of the Father. *God just isn't good or He wouldn't make you go through this. You'll have to take things into your own hands. Why don't you jump off the temple and just watch the people's eyes bug out when God sends His angels to rescue You! Or better yet, take my way. Just worship me today, and You'll be reigning over all the nations of the earth tomorrow! That will be much easier and quicker.*

God is not good, and He will not reward me when I diligently seek Him. I am in a terrible marriage and I want out. I need this money to get by even if it is dishonestly gained. *I can't trust God to reward me if I do things His way! His way makes no sense!* For our children in the classroom, it may simply be that *I don't believe that God loves me. If I don't look out for myself, I'm lost. If I don't gain the respect of my friends, I'm lost.* God is not going to take care of me. He is not going to reward me.

The third great lie of Satan like the second also deals with that second principle of Hebrews 11:6. But in this one, Satan involves his other great weapon, accusation. Satan tells me, *Yes God is good, but look what you did. Do you think God is going to reward the likes of you?* God is good, but I am not, so there is no way He will reward me. This is the lie that comes with guilt and fear and shame. This was the very lie Judas Iscariot believed as he went out and hung himself after throwing the money he earned for his betrayal back to the priests. And this is the lie so many of us believe once we have fallen to temptation. *After all God is just. How could He ever receive such a filthy lump of coal as I am?* Because, oh beloved one, God knows how to turn a lump of coal into a diamond! He saw in you a treasure for which He was willing to give all He had. He paid your price! He went to the cross to die for you. You don't think He paid all that only to throw you in the garbage can afterward, do you? It is in His care that you shall become the precious gem you were created to be.

These, then, are Satan's three great lies, and if we wish to achieve our goals of practical discipleship as situations arise in our classrooms, we must work to dispel them. God does not exist! God is not good! And God is good, but I am not, and He would never condescend to reward me even if I did seek Him. Which of these lies do the kids in your classroom believe? How can you best work to subvert those lies of Satan? How can you work to open their spiritual eyes? The truth must simply shine through our lives as Christian school teachers for the glory of our Father and the salvation of the souls of those little ones that sit in our classrooms.

Reflection: Are you acting like a true full-time soldier of Christ? Where do you fall short? In what areas do you need to improve to become a more effective soldier? Which of the five pillars is your weakest? Why? What steps can you take today to overcome this weakness? Write down all your thoughts for later reference.

IV. A Culture of Grace

We have spent the first three chapters of this book building a foundation for a Bible-centered plan of practical discipleship to replace the standard reward / punishment disciplinary plans we all grew up under. We have spoken of the basic function of the teacher in a paracletic roll as a coach to admonish, motivate, and teach her children in their battle against sin. We have presented the eight fundamental questions of life which allow us to counsel our children from an eternal perspective and have compared that plan to the psychological theories that the world has to offer, limited as they are by our mortality. Finally, we have spoken of the spiritual warfare we must face in the classroom, examining how we become effective warriors and studying the identity and tactics of the enemy.

Now it is time to begin a discussion of the specific ways we can build a program of practical discipleship on top of that foundation. We will start with the implementation of a culture of grace.

Grace and the Law

Now in order to properly understand grace, we must first grasp the roll and function of the law. Of the law? But haven't we been freed from the dominion of the law? Consider the words of Jesus in Matthew 5:17-20:

> **Do not think that I came to abolish the Law or the Prophets; I did not come to abolish, but to fulfill. [18] For truly I say to you, until heaven and earth pass away not the smallest letter or stroke shall pass from the Law until all is accomplished. [19] Whoever then annuls one of the least of these commandments and teaches others to do the same shall be called least in the kingdom of heaven; but whoever keeps and teaches them, he shall be called great in the kingdom of heaven. [20] For I say to you that unless your righteousness**

surpasses that of the scribes and Pharisees, you will not enter the kingdom of heaven.

Now if we take this passage at face value it would seem to contradict what we have always been taught. Didn't Jesus fulfill the law? He did! But He still insists that not one letter shall pass away until heaven and earth pass away. He condemns whoever attempts to annul and to teach the annulment of the least commandment as the least in heaven and commends whoever keeps and teaches them as great in the kingdom of heaven. If Jesus' fulfilling of the law in effect nullified it, then what can we make of this statement? Certainly we must reassess what we have always believed!

Jesus goes on in this passage to explain practically just exactly what He means with a number of specific examples taken from the law. In verses 21 and 22 He tells us:

> **You have heard that the ancients were told 'YOU SHALL NOT COMMIT MURDER' and 'Whoever commits murder shall be liable to the court. ²² 'But I say to you that everyone who is angry with his brother shall be guilty before the court; and whoever says to his brother, 'You good-for-nothing,' shall be guilty before the supreme court; and whoever says, 'You fool,' shall be guilty enough to go into the fiery hell.**

Ouch! Further in verses 27-28 He tells us:

> **You have heard that it was said, 'YOU SHALL NOT COMMIT ADULTERY'; ²⁸ but I say to you that everyone who looks at a woman with lust for her has already committed adultery with her in his heart.**

Now from these verses, we can come to only one conclusion; far from canceling the law or making it obsolete, Jesus actually *enhanced* the law, making it stricter than ever! The law, as originally written, seemed only to consider external acts as violations, whereas Jesus internalized it to govern even the secret counsels of the heart that none ever see but the one who harbors them. *Now* you could experience hell fire without ever *doing* a single thing wrong, but just because your *thoughts* weren't right before God! What can we conclude from this? First, that any discipline plan that does not deal with the heart is simply not adequate to our purpose. Second, that we must recognize the law as still very much a part of God's plan for salvation and incorporate that knowledge into our plan for practical discipleship.

So does that mean we need to teach our children Old Testament Law? I used to think the many New Testament passages concerning the law did not apply to me. After all, didn't the Jerusalem counsel in Acts 15 decide that Gentiles need not observe the Law? The answer is yes and no. There are certainly aspects of the Jewish Law that the Gentile Christian need not observe, but in a deeper sense we are all born under the law. Paul makes this clear in Romans 2:12-16:

> **For all who have sinned without the Law will also perish without the Law and all who have sinned under the Law will be judged by the Law; [13] for it is not the hearers of the Law who are just before God, but the doers of the Law will be justified. [14] For when Gentiles who do not have the Law do instinctively the things of the Law, these not having the Law are a law to themselves [15] in that they show the work of the Law written in their hearts their conscience bearing witness and their thoughts alternately accusing or else defending them [16] on the day when, according to my gospel, God will judge the secrets of men through Christ Jesus.**

Here then is the point: Like it or not, each and every child who lives long enough to begin to relate to his fellow human beings has within his heart an inborn understanding of good and evil that results from the decision of our first parents to eat the fruit of the tree that would impart that knowledge. We all understand without anyone telling us that certain things are right and certain things are wrong, and when we willingly commit those things that are wrong, we are worthy of punishment. Therefore, we have all, in a very real sense, been born and raised under *the* law although not, strictly speaking, the law of Moses. We cannot escape dealing with this law that is within us. Even young children understand this. Even the worst of parents teaches this to his children. Even the worst of parents has endeavored to punish his child for what is wrong. Therefore the children in our classrooms very much understand the concept of the law. What runs contrary to all their worldly experience is grace!

Grace cannot exist apart from the Law. Grace only makes sense within the context of the Law. Grace means receiving what I don't deserve. Unless I understand the law, I cannot understand that I deserve anything *but* the good things God offers. Grace without the law is nothing but license. Grace means understanding you are forgiven, and if there is no Law, there is nothing for which anyone could possibly ever need to be forgiven.

We see this principal at work in the sin of King David with Bath Sheba as told in 2 Samuel 11-12. Walking on the roof of his palace one evening with all his armies off to war, David spotted a woman taking her ritual bath after her menstruation. Discovering she was the wife of one of his top officers, Uriah the Hittite, he called her to him anyway and had sexual relations with her. Despite the fact that she had just finished her menstruation, Bath Sheba became pregnant. David attempted to cover up his sin by calling Uriah home from battle hoping he would enjoy his wife for an evening before returning. When all his scheming failed, he sent Uriah back to war, ordering his generals to orchestrate his death by abandoning him in the heat of battle.

The plan worked! David immediately arranged to marry Bath Sheba and life went on for nearly a year. Finally, Nathan came to confront him. The prophet weaved a parable about a poor man with a single lamb he treated like a daughter and a wealthy man who stole, cooked, and ate it. The story contained no names, no dates, and no specific geographic location, in short, nothing to give it the semblance of truth. Any thoughtful listener would have followed up with a simple question: *What are you trying to tell me, Nathan?* But David was so blinded by his own sin he got completely caught up in the story. Enraged, he stormed, *As the LORD lives surely the man who has done this deserves to die.* In fact the Law does *not* prescribe death for the crime described in the parable, but rather a four-fold restoration, as David himself recognizes in the end. However, David *had* committed two capital crimes under the law, adultery, and murder. Nathan finally had to tell him directly *You are the man!* and in the moment that the prophet pronounced those fateful words, David found himself face to face with a death sentence pronounced by his own lips. He broke. *I have sinned against the LORD!* Then Nathan extended those wonderful words of grace: *The LORD also has taken away your sin; you shall not die.*

Later, David wrote Psalm 32, reflecting back on the incident.

How blessed is he whose transgression is forgiven, Whose sin is covered! [2] How blessed is the man to whom the LORD does not impute iniquity, And in whose spirit there is no deceit! [3] When I kept silent about my sin, my body wasted away, Through my groaning all day long. [4] For day and night Your hand was heavy upon me; My vitality was drained away as with the fever heat of summer. Selah. [5] I acknowledged my sin to You And my iniquity I did not hide; I said, "I will confess my transgressions to the LORD"; And You forgave the guilt of my sin. Selah. (verses 1-5)

David's concealing of the sin for all those months had made him physically ill; his body wasted, and his vitality drained away. He says the hand of the Lord was heavy on him, but might *we* not say that it was the weight of the law? David knew what he deserved for his sin, but for nearly a year he tried to hide from it. When finally he did confess it, grace came like a ray of light piercing the black oppressive shadow of the law. The full forgiveness of God released him from the terrible weight he bore. As we can see, this grace could never have entered the picture were David not first heavily afflicted by the law. The law itself gave grace its power and indeed its very meaning.

Surprised by Grace

In our world defined by the rigid order of the law, grace enters in an astonishing and refreshing way. Numerous New Testament examples demonstrate the surprise generated by grace that comes as unexpectedly as it is unlooked for. We begin with the story of that wee little tax collector Zacchaeus from the opening verses of Luke 19.

As a Jewish tax collector for the Roman government, Zacchaeus was seen as a traitor to his own people. He had learned to survive harsh rejection by putting on a tough exterior. But at the same time he was consumed by resentment that caused him to scruple even less about cheating those that despised him. Now Zacchaeus had heard whispers about this prophet Jesus. He'd even noticed that a couple of people had started treating him more kindly after their encounter with Him on business trips to Galilee. He'd looked on those changes with the suspicion that came so naturally to his position but he'd never been able to catch them in any hypocrisy. His curiosity piqued, the tax collector decided he would just like to get a quick glimpse of the prophet one day when He was passing through town. Now the crowds were quite thick, and, being of small stature, Zacchaeus climbed up a few branches of a tree to see over them. As the Lord approached He did something completely unexpected. Looking over the heads of the multitude, He directed his gaze straight at Zacchaeus. "Zacchaeus!" How did the Lord know his name? "Come over here. I wondered if I might eat at your home today." The tax collector was flabbergasted and honored beyond belief by the Lord's attention. Enthusiastically, he took the Master to his home and prepared a huge banquet. He was struck by the Lord's simple, kind demeaner, and wonder grew in him as he observed the kind Teacher throughout the afternoon. By the end of the day, he was a new man. "Lord, half of my possessions I am giving to the poor, and if I have extorted anything from anyone, I am giving back four times as much. " Now there is no indication that Zacchaeus left his profession that day as Matthew before him had done. But certainly, if he indeed remained a tax collector, he did it with a decidedly different spirit from that day forward.

We might also contemplate the woman from John 8 caught, as the Pharisees told Jesus, in the very act of adultery.

That day that woman was worried about much more than the humiliating experience of being dragged naked before mocking crowds through the streets; the law of Moses commanded her death, and while this law was seldom enforced, there was most certainly death in the eyes of her captors and the crowds. And they were taking her to Jesus to ask His opinion on the matter! Now the young prophet was known to be kind and compassionate, but surely not even He could countenance the life she had lived! How her heart sank when she heard the Master siding, as she expected, with the Pharisees. But wait! Jesus threw in a bit of a caveat. *He who was without sin should cast the first stone!* No doubt this whole crowd would be clamoring over who merited the privilege! She lay sobbing, her shamed head buried in the sand. But that first stone never came. Little by little, she heard the noise of the crowd diminish. What was going on? She finally looked up when she felt a garment being thrown over her bare shoulders. The first thing she saw was the gently smiling face of the

Master who stood bent down over her with His hand extended. "Woman where are they? Does no one condemn you?" He asked. Confused, she looked around but could see none but the kind faces of Jesus' disciples. "No one, Lord." And Jesus said "I do not condemn you either. Go. From now on sin no more." (Verses 10-11) Expecting the full weight of the law to fall over her head at any moment, oh, the exhilarating freedom she felt when she was able to walk away to the home only moments before she thought she would never see again!

Then we present the woman at the well of John 4.

Approaching the well at midday, she was already a little weary of the day's work. Most women went to the well in the morning, but she didn't get along with other women. She just didn't need the eye rolls and the jocular conversations that abruptly ceased whenever she approached. No, it was just better she went to the well later in the day.

Looking forward, she saw a man sitting there. Well, that wasn't exactly a welcome prospect, but a good Samaritan wayfarer was often easily won by her casual flirtation. Maybe it wouldn't be so bad! But approaching yet a little closer, she realized he was a Jewish man. She groaned within herself. That couldn't be good! The best she could hope for was an upturned nose and a scornful ignorance. She hoped he wouldn't condescend to speak to her. Nothing good could come of that for as much as the Jews hated the Samaritans. Still, whatever might his attitude be toward her ethnicity, at least he wouldn't know about…

As she approached the man's eyes turned toward her and watched her intently. She was starting to feel quite uncomfortable with this situation in a rather unexpected way. Finally, the man spoke "Would you be so good as to give me a bit of water!"

Now of all the scenarios she might have imagined, this was certainly not one of them! And He spoke so warmly and courteously! What was He up to? She looked up at Him. The warmth in His eyes seemed genuine enough. Still, she just wasn't sure. "How is it that You ask me for a drink of water? Don't You know You're in Samaria?"

The man didn't look offended or at all surprised by her reaction. "If you knew who I am, you would have asked Me, and I would have given you *living* water to drink!"

What kind of words were these? What kind of bologna was He trying to feed her? "Look, You obviously have nothing to draw with. What are You talking about? Do You think You are somehow greater than our Father Jacob who dug this well and drank from it along with his sons and his cattle?"

The man smiled. It was a disarming smile truly! He nodded toward the well. "No, not this water. Whoever drinks this water will just get thirsty again in a little while. No, the water I offer you is the kind that will satisfy your thirst forever. The water that I give you will become a well springing up from within you to eternal life!"

The man certainly looked like He believed what He said. His eyes fairly glowed. Still, it was time to call His bluff. "Please, give me some of this water so I don't have to come back here and draw again. It's hard work you know?"

"Go call your husband!"

Well, she hadn't expected that response, but what of it? It just showed His ignorance! "I haven't got a husband."

"There you spoke truly. You don't have a husband. You have had five husbands, but the man you've got now isn't your husband."

Her mouth fell open. He *did* know! But how could he? Most people in the village didn't even know there had been five! Most had lost count or hadn't known her that long. After all, self-respecting people didn't hang around her much. "Sir, I perceive you are a prophet!" she gasped out. She scrambled for something to say to shore up her battered defenses. Finally, she grasped it, "Look, our fathers always said that this mountain was the proper place to worship, but you Jews always speak of Jerusalem. Who is right before Yahweh?"

The man smiled *so* warmly and looked straight into her eyes as he approached her and took her by the hand. "Believe me the time is coming when it won't be the one or the other. You Samaritans worship what you don't really know and we Jews worship what we know because salvation comes from the Jews. Still, pretty soon true worshippers of Yahweh won't worship Him necessarily either here nor in Jerusalem, but they will all worship Him in Spirit and in truth."

She turned her head away and her eyes filled with tears of bitterness, finally released. There was no deceit in this man and no con man could speak as He spoke. She knew she was in the presence of a holy man. Could it possibly be…? With her head down, she spoke of a hope that had been buried deep within her for years and that she had almost forgotten, "I know our Messiah is coming some day, and that He will declare all things to us!"

The man looked down and touched her chin lifting it up. "I who am speaking to you am He!"

A burst of joy exploded in her which she could not contain. At that moment, also, she saw another group of men, apparently friends of this Messiah, approaching. She felt a sudden urge to run; not to flee, but to go and... "Don't go away, please! I have to go tell everybody what I have seen!"

And thus, we see the surprising nature of grace as it first encroaches our law-ordered lives. And this same principal follows also with children. Paul Tripp tells the story of his pastor-brother Ted when a livid father brought his son to him after church one day. After he sat them down in his office the father turned to his son, "Now tell him what you did!" The son produced two dollars from his pocket and sheepishly confessed he had stolen it from the offering plate.

At that point Ted did something the little boy, who lived under the law, could never have expected. "Wow, you should be very happy! Jesus must love you very, very much" he said tenderly "because He allowed your father to see what you did and bring you to me. You see Jesus doesn't want you to become a thief, and He did all this to make sure you don't become one."

Upon hearing this, the boy began to cry and pulled out another twenty dollars from his pocket. Grace had won the day!

Similarly, Ken Sande of Peacemaker fame tells the story of how he pulled his young daughter out of a disciplinary situation and sat her down. "Honey, what do you think Jesus would say if He were here right now?"

"Don't provoke your brother!" she said with obvious annoyance, toting the line of the law.

"Well honey, I'm sure Jesus didn't want you to do that, but I think what He would do is tell you that He loves you so very much that He was willing to die for you because you do things like that."

Tears welled up in the little girl's eyes, and she said, "Daddy pray for me that God would help me behave myself better."

I myself had a moment like that with one of my kids when she was young, although I can't claim to have handled it quite as well as Ted Tripp and Ken Sande. One day, my wife and I bought two of those cheap balloon balls for our two very young children.

Back in the car on the way home, though the balls were identical, my daughter noticed a small defect in hers and complained loudly. "The paint on my ball is wearing off!"

I knew what she would do! When we got home their mother had them write their names on the balls. I picked up the ball with her name on it and handed it to her brother, "Here is your ball."

"That's not his ball, that's mine!" she said.

"No, it isn't, see, the paint is still good on this ball, but it's wearing a bit on the other one. That ball belongs to you."

I spoke very calmly and never raised my voice or uttered the first word of reproach, but my daughter, who must have been about five years old at the time, began to cry. Now if I had had the wisdom then that I do now, I probably would have told her something about how much Jesus loved her, but as it was I said not another word and just let God speak to her. That was the last time in her life that I believe my daughter ever told a deliberate lie. Years later, her high school observed a tradition of honoring one student each month that best exemplified a particular virtue. My daughter won the award during the month of honesty.

Applying Grace in the Classroom

Before we open the theme of this section, let us note Jesus' teaching in Luke 5:31-32. *It is not those who are well who need a physician, but those who are sick. I have not come to call the righteous, but sinners to repentance.*" Just as those who are not sick do not need doctors also those who have not been condemned do not need grace. Now all are condemned by the law, but just as those who do not know they are sick will not likely seek doctors, neither will those who refuse to recognize that they stand condemned, seek grace. Nevertheless, for those of us who work in evangelistic schools and not primarily with Christian families, there can be no doubt that our students, downtrodden and outcast as they quite often are, are exactly the kind of people that Jesus came to save. That they are also children makes it all that much more certain that they are primary objects of His compassion. Thus, we *must* provide this environment of grace in our classrooms.

Now that we have explored the concept of grace biblically and have a better understanding of just what it is and how it works, let us consider the ways in which we may apply it by turning disciplinary situations in the classroom into opportunities for practical discipleship. The best place to start is with a biblical example in which Jesus faced a situation with his disciples that looks very much like situations we might face in the classroom.

Let us look at Mark 9:33-37:

> **They came to Capernaum; and when He (Jesus) was in the house, He began to question them (his disciples), "What were you discussing on the way?" [34] But they kept silent for on the way they had discussed with one another which of them was the greatest.**

Now let us stop for the moment right there and pretend we don't know what happens next. Why didn't the disciples answer Jesus' question? They had been discussing who would be the greatest in the Kingdom of heaven! The parallel Scripture in Luke 9:46 uses the word *argument*. The discussion had likely gotten a bit heated. Now they weren't guilty of a serious crime from a human standpoint, but tempers here may still have been just a little warm, and they knew without being told that their behavior would not meet Jesus' approval and were embarrassed. What did they expect from Him? Probably a humiliating verbal rebuke! I probably would have obliged them. But Jesus did not give them that kind of reaction.

> **[35] Sitting down, He called the twelve and said to them, "If anyone wants to be first, he shall be last of all and servant of all." [36] Taking a child, He set him before them and, taking him in His arms, He said to them, [37] "Whoever receives one child like this in My name receives Me; and whoever receives Me does not receive Me but Him who sent Me."**

Rather than rebuking, Jesus actually affirmed their desire to be great in the Kingdom of God, but they were going about it all wrong! *If you really want to be the greatest, then be the exact opposite while you are here on this earth.* In the parallel scripture in Matthew 18:3-4, He says: *Truly I say to you unless you are converted and become like children, you will not enter the kingdom of heaven. Whoever then humbles himself as this child, he is the greatest in the kingdom of heaven.* "Be like this little child who doesn't pretend to be greater than any of you," He says, "and receive children like this and I will consider it as if you were receiving Me directly."

Oh that we might learn to take moments when those flaws in the hearts of our children are so keenly displayed and turn them into heart-mending, teaching moments as Jesus did!

But what else might we say about this? I look at the example of the Canaanite or Syrophoenician woman's encounter with Jesus. As this woman pestered Jesus to heal her demon-possessed daughter and Jesus continually ignored her, the disciples became irritated and asked Him to send her away. Instead, Jesus looked her straight in the eye and said, *I was sent only to the lost sheep of the house of Israel. It is not good to take the children's bread and throw it to the dogs.* Did He just call her a dog? However, Jesus knew the hearts of all He met. I can just imagine the broad grin that slowly spread over his face followed by roaring laughter as she answered him, *Yes Lord; but even the dogs feed on the crumbs which fall from their master's table.*

Because grace, in its most effective form, surprises us, there can be no absolute formula as to how it is dispensed. After all, such a formula would not be surprising. Sometimes, it simply takes divine creativity powered by the wisdom imparted by the Holy Spirit to a teacher who is fully in tune and constantly listening for that still small voice of God speaking into the everyday moments of life. As James 1:5 says: *But if any of you lacks wisdom, let him ask of God who gives to all generously and without reproach, and it will be given to him.* However, there is one more absolutely indispensable ingredient that a teacher must obtain in order to become a fountain of grace and we find it properly displayed in the story of the rich young ruler in Mark 10.

This young man came up to Jesus and asked Him how he might obtain eternal life. Jesus gave the standard answer about following the commandments and even specified a number of them. The young man was not satisfied, *Teacher I have kept all these things from my youth up.* In the parallel scripture of Matthew 19:20 he adds, *What am I still lacking?* Here is the key. Verse 21 (in Mark 10 NIV) says: *Jesus looked at him and loved him.* Hardly can grace be imparted through a vessel that is not filled with Christ's love. As we pray for wisdom, let us also pray that God would give us an indomitable love for those children that He has placed in our care.

After having said all of this, there are, without question, certain practices that should season our daily handling of every discipline case that comes before us, so let me just, in closing, give a few suggestions.

First, begin every disciplinary meeting with prayer. It is difficult for two children who had just come to blows in the playground not to soften at least a little as you present their case before God before even working it. That initial prayer can be a powerful soothing agent to open the heart of an angry child.

Second, listen intently! A child is much more likely to recognize his own sin and confess it if he feels you have heard his side of the story and are not judging him in ignorance. On the contrary there is nothing that more embitters a child than to be punished when he feels he has *not* been heard.

Third, remind that child that Jesus loves him and that you do to. These words can never be spoken too often, and they will comfort the child in those difficult times.

Fourth, tell the story of something you have done that resembles what the child did. Often, we say that we are sinners, but beyond the saying, we often don't act like we really believe it. Seeing that vulnerability in the adults of his life can give a good measure of hope to a child who has difficulty overcoming his own sin.

Finally, smile. Good humor can truly disarm some mortally tense situations. I recall a time when two girls in my office came in furious at each other. I may have imitated one or the other that got them both giggling just a little. Then in mock fury I pounded my fist on my desk and yelled, "We're supposed to be fighting here!" Any pretense of enmity dissolved in that moment.

I am also reminded of the beautiful story of the famous Methodist circuit rider, Peter Cartwright. In one of his revival meetings several young men were lounging over on the women's side of the meeting, flirting with some attractive girls there. Peter announced that the meeting was about to start and asked them to find their seats. Most obeyed, but a couple tried to duck down and escape the evangelist's notice. Cartwright, who was known as the two-fisted preacher, having been somewhat of a brawler before his conversion, would have none of it. "You, the young man in the overalls, he called out, unless you've got a skirt underneath those things, go over to the men's side." The young man hurried out of the meeting, greatly humiliated.

That evening, as God's providence would have it, Cartwright found himself dining in a company that included the boy's father who had not been at the meeting that morning but was enraged at the treatment of his son. "Why, if you weren't such a coward, I would challenge you to a duel!" fumed the injured father. The quietly dining Cartwright answered, "If you challenge me to a duel, I will accept."

The man's anger boiled over. "All right, I challenge you." A tense silence settled over the room as Cartwright only quietly continued his dinner. After a moment the circuit rider said, "As the one challenged, I suppose that I have the right to choose the weapon?"

"Yes, of course," said his challenger.

"Well, let's just go out into that cornfield and cut a couple of stalks and have it out with them."

The comment was so absurd, so unexpected, that the silence continued for several seconds afterward until finally the father laughed a nervous laugh and the tension was broken. That man came to Christ that very evening.

Reflection: Think of a time when you were surprised by grace or when you surprised someone else by grace. What impact did it have on you or on the person who received it? Think of ways in which you can create in your own classroom a culture of grace. Write down all your thoughts for later reference.

V. Biblical Consequences

In building a culture of grace, we were forced to recognize that the law still governs our lives and to it grace owes its very existence. What then does this imply about consequences in the classroom? What consequences does grace suggest? Where does the law fit in?

Parental Authority

Before we begin to study the application of consequences in the classroom, we must first note that the Bible specifically grants authority to discipline children to their parents. Let us first look at that foundational passage to the Jewish faith in Deuteronomy 6:

> **Now this is the commandment the statutes and the judgments which the LORD your God has commanded me to teach you that you might do them in the land where you are going over to possess it [2] so that you and your son and your grandson might fear the Lord your God to keep all His statutes and His commandments which I command you all the days of your life and that your days may be prolonged. [3] O Israel you should listen and be careful to do it that it may be well with you and that you may multiply greatly just as the LORD the God of your fathers has promised you in a land flowing with milk and honey.**
>
> **[4] Hear O Israel! The LORD is our God, the LORD is one! [5] You shall love the LORD your God with all your heart and with all your soul and with all your might.**
>
> **[6] These words which I am commanding you today shall be on your heart. [7] You shall teach them diligently to your sons and shall talk of them when you sit in your house and when you walk by the way and when you lie down and when you rise up. [8] You shall bind them as a sign on your hand and they shall be as frontals on your forehead. [9] You shall write them on the doorposts of your house and on your gates. (Verses 1-9)**

Note first that the law was to be a multi-generational covenant passed down from Father to son that *you and your son and your grandson might fear the Lord your God to keep all His statutes and His commandments which I command you.* Note also how it was to be a constant topic of conversation between parents and their children from the early morning until the late evening *You shall teach them diligently to your sons and shall talk of them when you sit in your house and when you walk by the way and when you lie down and when you rise up.* .

And not only the Law of Moses affirms the authority of parents in the discipline of their children. Ephesians 6:4 commands: *Fathers, do not provoke your children to anger, but bring them up in the discipline and instruction of the Lord.* Proverbs 1:9 speaks specifically of the instruction of both father and mother: *Hear, my son, your father's instruction, And do not forsake your mother's teaching; Indeed, they are a graceful wreath to your head, And ornaments about your neck.* (verses 1:9) From the context of the Proverbs, we understand very well that this instruction and teaching does not speak of mathematics or business or anything else, but to live in such a way as to please the Father and to honor one's fellow men. Even more to the point, we find in 6:20-23:

> **My son, observe the commandment of your father, And do not forsake the teaching of your mother; [21] Bind them continually on your heart; Tie them around your neck. [22] When you walk about, they will guide you; When you sleep, they will watch over you; And when you awake, they will talk to you. [23] For the commandment is a lamp, and the teaching is light; And reproofs for discipline are the way of life.**

Note the similarities in this passage and Deuteronomy 6 with which we began the chapter. Proverbs 6 says: *Bind them continually on your heart; Tie them around your neck.* And Deuteronomy 6 says: *You shall bind them as a sign on your hand, and they shall be as frontals on your forehead.*

However, the authority and responsibility for specifically the parents to discipline is even more *understood* and taken for granted in the Bible than it is *commanded.* Consider the words of Hebrews 12:

and you have forgotten the exhortation which is addressed to you as sons "MY SON, DO NOT REGARD LIGHTLY THE DISCIPLINE OF THE LORD NOR FAINT WHEN YOU ARE REPROVED BY HIM; [6] FOR THOSE WHOM THE LORD LOVES, HE DISCIPLINES, AND HE SCOURGES EVERY SON WHOM HE RECEIVES."

[7] It is for discipline that you endure; God deals with you as with sons; for what son is there whom his father does not discipline? [8] But if you are without discipline of which all have become partakers, then you are illegitimate children and not sons. [9] Furthermore, we had earthly fathers to discipline us and we respected them; shall we not much rather be subject to the Father of spirits and live? [10] For they disciplined us for a short time as seemed best to them, but He disciplines us for our good so that we may share His holiness. [11] All discipline for the moment seems not to be joyful, but sorrowful; yet to those who have been trained by it, afterwards it yields the peaceful fruit of righteousness. (verses 5-11)

Now such words as: *God deals with you as with sons; for what son is there whom his father does not discipline?* make the author's view perfectly clear. We don't even need to command parents to discipline their children. This is simply what they do, and the Bible affirms this by telling us that when God disciplines us, He is treating us as a father does his beloved children.

The practical application of all this to our theme is that a Christian school operates in subjection to and as an extension of parental authority. In no way are we to usurp this authority. We may believe that certain parents are unfit to discipline their children properly, but this is a reason to educate them, not to take their authority away by failing to communicate and handling problems ourselves. This is also why school suspension is an appropriate consequence for more serious offenses; it puts the discipline of the child in the proper hands. The Dominican *Normas de Convivencia* code for school discipline states that all suspensions must be handled in the school environment where the institution provides a space outside the classroom for the child to do his work *supervised by his teacher and his family*. Even the Dominican *Normas* puts the child in the right hands. The teacher is there to supervises his schoolwork, but the parent, to provide the discipline. When I have applied this consequence to a child, often parents have told me they would simply prefer to keep their child home on the day of suspension. This is perfectly fine. The child remains in the right hands, and, contrary to what many have suggested, I have *never* had a child that has viewed the suspension as a day of vacation.

Punishments, Consequences of the Law

As we read in the previous chapter, the law is still very much in effect, and without it grace cannot exist. We have seen that the law demands discipline be applied to children by their parents, but just what is the nature of this discipline? Hebrews 12:11, which we quoted earlier, says: *All discipline for the moment seems not to be joyful but sorrowful; yet to those who have been trained by it, afterwards it yields the peaceful fruit of righteousness.* Clearly, according to the author of Hebrews, discipline hurts! This concept is expressed many times in the book of Proverbs:

13:24	**He who withholds his rod, hates his son** **But he who loves him, disciplines him diligently.**
19:18	**Discipline your son while there is hope,** **And do not desire his death.**
20:30	**Stripes that wound scour away evil,** **And strokes reach the innermost parts.**
22:15	**Foolishness is bound up in the heart of a child;** **The rod of discipline will remove it far from him.**
23:13-14	**Do not hold back discipline from the child,** **Although you strike him with the rod, he will not die.** **You shall strike him with the rod,** **And rescue his soul from Sheol.**
29:15	**The rod and reproof give wisdom,** **But a child who gets his own way brings shame to his mother.**
29:17	**Correct your son, and he will give you comfort;** **He will also delight your soul.**

The Bible unquestionably commends the use of punishments that physically hurt. However, while we believe that the authority of the teacher in a Christian school is an extension of this parental authority, we do *not* believe that this authority to physically punish children extends to the school. This is an area that remains firmly in the hands of the parents. However, the school *is* granted the right to apply corrective punishment that hurts in non-physical ways.

This, then, begs two questions; when? and what? The simple answer to when is when your law demands it. If the purpose of discipline is ultimately to lead a child to Christ and help him to grow, then it is absolutely essential that he understand the punishment is just. He should never be surprised by it as it should be well defined beforehand by your law. Nor should punishment normally be withheld him if he has earned it under your law.

Before we discuss what *kind* of punishments we should apply under our law, let us first consider the *purpose* for punishment. The absolute law of God says that the wages of sin is death. That is the punitive law that represents the demands of justice. This is *not* the law that we deal with in life's daily challenges. We observe a different law with a different purpose. Just what is this law? Let us consider Galatians 3:19-27:

> **Why the Law then? It was added because of transgressions, having been ordained through angels by the agency of a mediator until the seed would come to whom the promise had been made. [20] Now a mediator is not for one party only; whereas God is only one. [21] Is the Law, then, contrary to the promises of God? May it never be! For if a law had been given which was able to impart life, then righteousness would indeed have been based on law. [22] But the Scripture has shut up everyone under sin so that the promise by faith in Jesus Christ might be given to those who believe.**
>
> **[23] But before faith came, we were kept in custody under the law being shut up to the faith which was later to be revealed. [24] Therefore, the Law has become our tutor to lead us to Christ so that we may be justified by faith. [25] But now that faith has come, we are no longer under a tutor. [26] For you are all sons of God through faith in Christ Jesus. [27] For all of you who were baptized into Christ have clothed yourselves with Christ.**

Here we see both the purpose of the ancient Mosaic Law and the law of our classrooms. The Law was and is added *because of transgressions*. We as human beings need expressed limits to our behavior, and we need punishment as a device to establish those as true boundaries. Without punishment, they are mere suggestions and have no binding capacity over us at all. So, what exactly is the role of the law? The law serves as a tutor so that we might learn what God and our earthly authorities demand of us. Now since faith has come, we Christian school teachers are no longer under a tutor, but this is often *not* the case with the children we work with. Even those who are saved have only an immature faith. They are still in need of that tutor as Hebrews 12:11 so clearly expresses. That tutor will, when rightly applied, gradually guide them to a mature faith as they know and grow in Jesus Christ. Understanding, then, that our law serves as a tutor, we see that the punishments we inflict hold the purpose, not to satisfy justice, but to instruct with the end view of introducing our children to and forming them into the image of Christ.

The question as to what kind of punishments we should apply is a bit complicated and I will not presume there is any universal answer to it, but, generally speaking, it is appropriate to take privileges away from students, to take time from students at recess or even after school, or to give a student a failing grade. However, the consequences should fit the misdeed. Certainly, a student who has shown consistent irresponsibility should understand that he may not be allowed to play on the school basketball team. A child who cheats on a test should not expect to get credit for the test. Suspensions can also be a very effective consequence as we have mentioned earlier. If a student irresponsibly takes time away from the teacher, with fair warning, the teacher is justified in taking time away from him. However, taking recess away can be counter-productive, and she should be careful about doing it too often as children need that time to reduce their excess energy and stress.

We have already spoken of the inappropriateness of corporal punishments. Among other inappropriate punishments are writing sentences. This simply has very little corrective value to it. Corporate punishments are not anti-biblical as we see in the case of the battle of Ai where God allowed the entire Israelite army to be defeated and several dozen families to lose fathers because of one man's sin at Jericho. However, such actions are a perfect way to provoke resentment among the students who see themselves as innocent towards those they consider guilty and toward the teacher who inflicted the punishment. Corporate punishment should, therefore, be used sparingly and never with consequences that are too grave. Further, a student should not be excluded from the classroom as a punishment, isolating him from his peers and teachers, unless it is to place him into the hands of his parents for a very grave offense. I have seen teachers lock students that arrive late to class outside their rooms. What is the purpose for this? One of the great comforts of Christian living is that we may always run into the arms of our loving Father when we experience the suffering of His discipline. Teachers and faculty of a Christian school should likewise also always have their arms and offices open to their students, especially in the midst of disciplinary problems.

Before applying any punishment, several things should be taken into consideration. First, as we have already explained, punishment should be well defined beforehand such that a child knows the probable consequences before he receives them. Second, as we have also mentioned, significant punishments should never be applied until you have taken time to listen to the student. Finally, if a student does not learn from a particular punishment, it is inadvisable to repeat it four and five times. At that point it is time to try something new.

One more area we should look at before we close this section. What do we do with 1 Corinthians 5:5? *I have decided to deliver such a one to Satan for the destruction of his flesh so that his spirit may be saved in the day of the Lord Jesus.* Certainly, Paul did not intend this verse to speak of children and certainly he was not speaking of schools, but rather of the church. It would be completely incorrect for a church to expel a child from its midst, but a school is not a church. Sometimes, expulsion is necessary for the protection of the rest of our students, and a school has the authority and occasionally even the responsibility to do it. However, we should always do it with the hope that the student may be one day restored to Christ, and the school should be open to even restoring him as a student. If we truly believe in the transforming blood of Jesus Christ, we can do no less.

Taking off and Putting on, Consequences of Grace

Grace adds a completely new dimension to the concept of consequences for bad behavior. It teaches us to take off the old *and* put on the new. We tend to think of classroom discipline in somewhat monolithic terms—of merely stopping the things a child ought not do. However a truly rounded plan for practical discipleship teaches us not just to eliminate the old, bad behavior, but to replace it with something new and good. A person who has a genuine love of Jesus Christ will desire to do just that, and children who have been taught the truths of the Bible need it as well.

The concept of taking off the old and putting on the new is most fully developed in Ephesians 4 from verse 17 to the end:

> **So this I say and affirm together with the Lord, that you walk no longer just as the Gentiles also walk in the futility of their mind [18] being darkened in their understanding, excluded from the life of God because of the ignorance that is in them because of the hardness of their heart; [19] and they, having become callous, have given themselves over to sensuality for the practice of every kind of impurity with greediness. [20] But you did not learn Christ in this way [21] if indeed you have heard Him and have been taught in Him just as truth is in Jesus [22] that in reference to your former manner of life, you lay aside the old self which is being corrupted in accordance with the lusts of deceit [23] and that you be renewed in the spirit of your mind [24] and put on the new self which, in the likeness of God, has been created in righteousness and holiness of the truth.**
>
> **[25] Therefore, laying aside falsehood, SPEAK TRUTH, EACH ONE of you WITH HIS NEIGHBOR, for we are members of one another. [26] BE ANGRY, AND yet DO NOT SIN; do not let the sun go down on your anger, [27] and do not give the devil an opportunity. [28] He who steals must steal no longer; but rather he must labor, performing with his own hands what is good so that he will have something to share with one who has need. [29] Let no unwholesome word proceed from your mouth, but only such a word as is good for edification according to the need of the moment so that it will give grace to those who hear. [30] Do not grieve the Holy Spirit of God by whom you were sealed for the day of redemption. [31] Let all bitterness and wrath and anger and clamor and slander be put away from you along with all malice. [32] Be kind to one another, tender-**

hearted, forgiving each other just as God in Christ also has forgiven you.

Just not doing bad things leaves us irrelevant and invisible before the world. To simply strip a child of his old, sinful ways is to leave him spiritually naked. Righteous acts, on the other hand, clothe us in immaculate garments that turn worldly eyes. As Revelation 19:5 says: *It was given to her* (the church) *to clothe herself in fine linen, bright and clean; for the fine linen is the righteous acts of the saints.* And as you should have guessed by now, being clothed with the new does not just deal with the exterior. It's hard to feel like a homeless vagabond when dressed in a tuxedo. Putting on the new speaks also of being *renewed in the spirit of your mind.* When Christ gave his disciples His last supper, He did not stop with the bread that represented his body, the old, mortal part of His being. He also gave the wine that represented His life blood, a renovation to the old sacrificial system that forbade consumption of blood. Christianity does not speak merely of the death of our old sinful natures; it speaks of giving us new life as well. And this is basic to any true plan for practical discipleship. I learned the particularly important lesson of taking off the old and putting on the new when I took in, before my marriage, a young man who was struggling to leave the homosexual lifestyle in which he had been deeply entrenched. Taking off the old was a difficult enough task, but in doing so, this young man felt a profound sense of loss and struggled daily to find and put on his new identity in Jesus Christ. It was not easy! It meant a new relationship; it meant new lifestyle choices; it meant a new physical wardrobe; it meant literally a whole new life, and it was a life in which he often felt he did not well fit.

Fortunately, with children, who have a still-developing brain and are not nearly so deeply entrenched in an old sinful lifestyle, the changes are not profound and lie primarily in behavior. This particular passage gives us a number of very specific old things to take off and new things to put on in their stead. It tells us to take off falsehood and put on speaking the truth. It tells us to take off stealing and put on laboring with the hands in order to have enough to give to those who have need. It tells us to take off unwholesome words and put on speech that edifies. It tells us to take off bitterness, wrath, anger, clamor, slander, and malice and put on kindness, tender-heartedness, and forgiveness. Let us look at each of these four wardrobe changes in more detail and examine how they might be applied in the classroom.

The first of these changes is to take off falsehood and put on speaking the truth. When the truth is exposed after a child has been deliberately deceitful, it is not enough to simply receive that truth, we must strive to receive it *from his lips*. This means not merely his nod of assent after hearing the truth from someone else, but it encourages him to have the courage to make a full accounting of the truth for himself before all that he attempted to deceive. As a consequence of grace; putting on must not be by force. Through the process of counseling, we hope the child will willingly submit to tell the truth.

The second wardrobe change really suggests a radical idea. It says to take off stealing and put on laboring with the hands in order to have enough to give to those who have need. Under Old Testament Law after stealing it was not enough just to restore what one had taken. In Exodus 22:1 we find: *If a man steals an ox or a sheep and slaughters it or sells it, he shall pay five oxen for the ox and four sheep for the sheep.* Proverbs 6:30-31 goes even farther: *Men do not despise a thief if he steals, To satisfy himself when he is hungry; But when he is found, he must repay sevenfold; He must give all the substance of his house.* For the Christian, however, this giving back in excess does not come from obligation, but out of the willingness of the heart. In Luke 19 when Zacchaeus was converted, he volunteered to give back four times what he had unjustly taken. Certainly, this number was chosen from his knowledge of Old Testament Scripture, but it was required of him by no one. In the case of a child in the classroom, what would it look like to ask him to work an hour in the school in order to earn money to buy a candy bar or a small treat of some kind for the one from whom he stole? This would be a bold way to put a biblical principal to work in practical discipleship.

The third wardrobe change tells us to take off unwholesome words and put on speech that edifies. Every time we work through a disciplinary process involving unwholesome, insulting, or slanderous. language a child must be encouraged, not just to apologize for the bad, but to speak well about the person he slandered. This may also be done in written form so that the child has time to think through the words he is going to say and express them in a more polished way.

This will also help a child to see and appreciate the good points of the person he recently harmed with his words.

The final wardrobe change tells us to take off bitterness, wrath, anger, clamor, slander, and malice and put on kindness, tender-heartedness and forgiveness. This one speaks of changing the spiritual underclothes. It is not speaking of externals, but of true heart change and can never be forced as can those that deal in externals. The teacher must simply hold up a spiritual mirror to the child and confront him with it. Does he like the image he sees? Does he want to be a bitter angry child or would he prefer to be kind and forgiving? This may be a hard step for many children to take, but they must be challenged and invited to do it.

Certainly, the concept of taking off and putting on may and must be extended beyond these four wardrobe changes of Ephesians 4. Many other biblical examples may be cited which, although they might not use the same language, definitely do use the same concept of taking off the old and evil and putting on the new and just. The Christian school teacher must always ask where the principal of taking off and putting on leads in any particular disciplinary case. What to take off is usually obvious. Deciding what to put on sometimes takes a little more thought. In many cases, the correct answer may be to simply ask the child to repeat a situation, correcting the bad behavior this time around. If the child is a repeat offender of more or less the same sin, have him repeat it more than once. This will be the beginning of reprogramming his responses to help him better deal with life.

Taking off and putting on may be used in virtually any disciplinary situation of any import. It should even be used when the teacher determines that consequences of the law are in order as well.

Reflection: In finishing this chapter take some time to consider some situations in your classroom that you should apply the principal of taking off and putting on. Can you find a Bible verse that speaks to your situation? Write down your thought for future reference.

VI. The Essence of Practical Discipleship

Having studied now the concepts of grace and consequences in the last two chapters, it is time to walk through the specific format of practical discipleship counseling. How should we handle any given disciplinary situation? What steps are involved?

Take off Preaching and Put on Listening

What is the best way to reach the heart of a child? As teachers filled with worldly and spiritual wisdom, we tend to our natural default, our tongues. We have all kinds of sage advice to impart to the children in our care on virtually any topic, and we are just bursting for opportunities to share it. Unfortunately, all too often our profound sapience falls on all-too-deaf ears.

Now Jesus knew all men because He created them. He always knew the exact best words to most effectively minister to anyone He met, and He seldom ever shared the gospel in the same way twice. He told some, *Follow me and I will make you fishers of men.* He told another, *You must be born again of the Spirit.* He told another, *Go and sin no more.* He told another, *Go and sell all that you have, and you will have rewards in heaven, and come and follow Me.* Another, He offered living water. For another, He simply went to his home to dine and never opened His mouth to say another word. In most of these examples of personal evangelism, it is remarkable how little Jesus spoke. Except in the case of the intellectual Nicodemus, His words were generally very brief and to the point.

If Jesus resisted sermonizing in his personal ministry why are we Christian teachers so quick to embrace it? Furthermore, we lack Jesus' divine knowledge of our fellow man. For us to effectively minister to our children, we must take the time to know them and that implies just sitting down and listening—how much more so in the middle of a disciplinary situation! And the Scriptures bear out the importance of listening much and speaking little time and again. James 1:19 says: *This you know, my beloved brethren. But everyone must be quick to hear, slow to speak, and slow to anger.* Proverbs 17:28 tells us: *Even a fool, when he keeps silent, is considered wise; When he closes his lips, he is considered prudent.* More to the point, Proverbs 18:13 says: *He who gives an answer before he hears, It is folly and shame to him.* How many times have we, as teachers, fallen into that folly and shame?

Why, again, does James tell us in 3:1: *Let not many of you become teachers, my brethren, knowing that as such we will incur a stricter judgment?* Because being a teacher requires extensive use of the tongue. It is in the nature of those inclined to be teachers to forget the old adage of what it means to have two ears and only one mouth. Indeed, judging by how much they talk, some teachers seem to perceive themselves to have an altogether different anatomy. At the same time, being a good listener does require a *prudent* use of the tongue. Proverbs 20:5 tells us: *A plan in the heart of a man is like deep water, But a man of understanding draws it out.* Does not it take a man or woman of understanding to draw plans from the heart of a child as well? As this proverb implies, being a good listener requires learning how to pose questions that will truly draw our students out. So just what kind of questions do we need to ask?

Ken Sande, founder of the Peacemakers ministry, speaks of a condition he calls an amygdala hijacking. The amygdala is a tiny globe within the human brain that serves as the emergency response center. It is programmed to take over the brain in moments of extreme emotion so as to react quickly to situations which call for possibly life-saving action. Both its size and its function would suggest that its range of options is limited, and indeed, that is the case. When the amygdala is in control in the human adult, it chooses among three possible courses of action: fight, freeze, or flee. It is no more complicated than that. A child, however, will not freeze in emergency situations. At moments of high emotion, he is incapable of doing anything but fight or flee. (Truthfully, I think the teacher's amygdala is limited to only the fight option.) Sande suggests the use of the question, *What emotion are you feeling right now?* Studies have shown that this question is effective in reactivating a hijacked brain, thereby opening the path to a solution.

Once the child is calm and capable once again of rational thought, Paul Tripp suggests these five questions.

1. What happened?
2. What were your thoughts and emotions when it happened?
3. What did you do in response?
4. Why did you do it? What were you trying to accomplish?
5. What were the results?

These questions can lead a child to evaluate his own conduct. Did he have a good reason for responding the way that he did? Was his response appropriate and likely to achieve his goals? Did he get what he was after? The answer to these questions is, in all likelihood, *no,* or you would not be in the middle of the conversation to begin with. Of course, that is usually easy for a teacher to see, but the child himself needs help. This kind of question, when prudently applied, can help a child develop patterns of evaluating his own actions and modifying them to produce better results in the future.

Take off Accusing and Put on Admonishing

It certainly is not the first question that a counselor / teacher should ask, but it is the most important, and all our efforts ought to move toward asking it at the proper time. *What did you do wrong?* Or perhaps it would be better to phrase it, *What do you think you did wrong?* Our first instinct as teachers and parents and human beings is to *tell* a child what he did wrong, but this is absolutely the worst course to take. Who is properly called the Accuser of the brethren, anyway? Do we really want to give the devil the day off? Maybe I don't see myself so much as the accuser as the judge. Is that where I really want to be? A judge issues justice. Am I capable of issuing true justice? It is the Father's job to judge, not mine. Or perhaps I may think that I'm only trying to bring conviction to the child. Is that my job? That is the job of the Holy Spirit.

Well, if I don't want to take the devil's, the Father's, nor the Holy Spirit's job, what exactly is my job? This is a question, we answered in chapter 2. My job is to admonish, encourage, motivate, and teach. My job is to be a paraclete, a coach that walks alongside the child, moving him to godliness. Accusing, judging, and convicting are simply not part of the job description. Once we have gone through the process together of examining everything so that I as the counselor understand what happened and that the child understands and has evaluated his own actions, it is time to face the question of sin and repentance. I do not need to tell the child what he has done wrong. He has probably known from the beginning, but he should definitely have a good idea by now. Asking him the question, *what do you think you did wrong,* gives him an opportunity to morally evaluate his own actions. It gives the Holy Spirit the opportunity to work within him to help him confess openly and without coercion exactly how he may have sinned.

But what happens if he doesn't admit to all that he did wrong? What do I do then? There is still no good reason to accuse, but there is occasion to get more specific. If a child admits to having done something wrong but leaves something out you feel he ought to admit to it is perfectly reasonable to ask him this follow-up question. *What about this? Do you think that this was correct?* Normally, the child will immediately recognize his oversight and admit that, yes, this too was incorrect.

But what happens if a child did ten things wrong and confesses to eight of them but adamantly insists that he did not do the other two? What do I do then? Let it alone! My counsel is to work with what the child has given you. At this point, it is very easy to enter into a confrontational mode that is unlikely to have a positive result. It is best for the teacher to work with the eight things the child has confessed to and lead him through a process of repentance for these things. The child is usually willing to humble himself concerning these things, and it is usually enough to restore relations in a very satisfactory way.

And what happens if the child is unwilling to confess to anything? Well, now we are entering an area which I'm not sure I've ever seen in my twenty-five years of experience in a Christian school, and if I have seen it once, I've not seen it again. There is a big difference between a child who, on a particular occasion, refuses to take responsibility for the wrong he did and one who *never* takes responsibility. Our goals for classroom discipline are evangelism and discipleship. Discipleship is long-term and not defined by a single incident. If a child, on one particular occasion, refuses to take responsibility for the wrong he does two options present themselves. First of all, we can choose just to let it go. It may not be worth the trouble, or it is possible that we are evaluating the situation incorrectly and that the child truly is innocent. Second, we can choose to revisit the incident a day or two later. By that time, a child may have a different perspective. If a child regularly refuses to take responsibility for significant offenses, then it is time to call in the cavalry. The problem is bigger than what the individual teacher is capable of facing alone, and, as a team, you must develop a plan to work with the child. Still, in all my years of experience, I must say that if you go through the process of listening and asking questions in an effective way, situations where the child is unwilling to confess to any wrongdoing shall be considerably less than few and far between and trending toward non-existent!

Applying the Bible

Now it is time for us as teachers to put on our didaskalos hats. Let us begin with this all-important scripture:

> **For the word of God is living and active and sharper than any two-edged sword and piercing as far as the division of soul and spirit of both joints and marrow and able to judge the thoughts and intentions of the heart. [13] And there is no creature hidden from His sight, but all things are open and laid bare to the eyes of Him with whom we have to do. Hebrews 4:12-13**

Based on this passage, are the Scriptures more properly used as a hammer or a surgical knife? All too often, they have been used as a hammer. They have been used to abuse and to enslave, instead of to heal and liberate. One-hundred-eighty-year-old images of southern planters preaching, *Slaves, obey your masters,* come immediately to mind. I have heard of a Christian school that, for a time, prohibited its teachers from using the Scriptures. The Bible was left exclusively to the counselors. I was shocked, but that school had experienced incidents of teachers using the Scriptures as a hammer to beat a child and tell him what a low-life sinner he was. My friends, such a teacher has no place in a Christian school! Perhaps, she may be instructed in a better way, but if she has and will receive no better understanding of grace than that, then she is not a proper representative of Christ before her students.

A hammer serves blows to the exterior of the body and has no capacity to heal and fix, but a surgical knife penetrates to the interior and lays bare the malignancy inside. The Scriptures should be used with the finesse and precision of a surgeon removing a cancerous tumor from the body. They should never be used to accuse or condemn. They should not be used to teach a child something he already knows. For instance, a child caught stealing will hardly be helped by a visit to the ten commandments. This child already knows perfectly well that stealing is against God's law and doesn't need it to be taught over again. What he needs is a more subtle teaching. He needs a teaching that will guide him to a better path, such as Ephesians 4:28: *He who steals, must steal no longer; but, rather, he must labor, performing with his own hands what is good so that he will have something to share with one who has need.* The Scriptures should be used thus to expose sin and to show a better way, not only to take off, but to put on as well.

Before closing this chapter, I would like to introduce you to two of my favorite scriptures which I have applied time and again in disciplinary situations. The first is Proverbs 15:1: *A gentle answer turns away wrath, But a harsh word stirs up anger.* Since a good percentage of our sin uses the tongue as its instrument, this is a verse with which one can get a lot of mileage. Many times, I have pulled it out and given it to a child to read. I may ask him what the verse means to him. Then, I will ask which of the two terms, the gentle answer or the harsh word, his words most closely resembled. When he invariably acknowledges that his was a harsh word, I ask him *According to this verse what kind of reaction can you expect when you speak that way?* When he answers, I may ask, *Is that what happened this time?*

The other is the passage from Daniel 1. I always need to explain the background so as to be more precise in my application.

Daniel was brought from Jerusalem as a hostage, along with his three friends, to Babylon where they were taken into the royal academy to be trained in the wisdom of the greatest nation on earth. Then we read verse 8: *But Daniel made up his mind that he would not defile himself with the king's choice food or with the wine which he drank; so he sought permission from the commander of the officials that he might not defile himself.* Daniel had a choice, and either option was bad. He could either offend God by eating the king's food or offend the king by not eating it. Nevertheless, Daniel, who was quite a young man at the time, perhaps the same age as some of my middle-school students, found a third way. I am always reminded at this point of the popular song, *God will make a way when it seems there is no way.* I use this passage to speak to a youth who has been defiant to a teacher for some perceived injustice. Daniel had much nobler motives than probably most of my students, but from this story, we see a fine example of prudence in speech and reliance upon God which can shine as a light to our young pupils who may think at times that they are wiser than they are.

Reflection: In this chapter we have spoken of three garments we as teachers may need to take off and put on. We spoke of taking of preaching and putting on listening. We spoke of taking off accusing and putting on admonishing. Finally, we spoke of taking off using the Bible as a hammer and putting on using it as a surgical knife. Which of these three speaks most to you? How can you apply it in your classroom? Write down your reflections.

VII. Applying the Scriptures

In this chapter, I hope to accomplish two primary goals. First of all, I want to mold all that we have spoken of so far and particularly in the last chapter into a structured form, into a process which we may follow when applying practical discipleship in disciplinary situations. I would like to mention at the outset that this process may seem to require an enormous amount of time, and it may, indeed, on occasion. Still, teachers represent the front line in applying these principles and procedures and should be well familiar with them although in practice the more difficult cases will often fall to counselors. Second, I wish to give a series of scriptures that may be applied to different classroom situations to give the teacher a bag of tools, so to speak, to access when common classroom difficulties arise.

Preparing the Soil

Of course, applying the Scriptures is not the first thing that a teacher should do when working with a child for disciplinary purposes. Before the process can even begin, we must coax a child out of a state of amygdala hijacking as we developed in the last chapter. Often the question, *What emotions are you feeling right now?* is the way to begin. Then we set the atmosphere with a prayer and a smile and with a reminder to the child that God loves him. Once he is calmed down and reasonably comfortable, the process may begin.

A rough guideline for the actual procedure might be organized into four steps described by the acronym, ICAM. The steps are:

1. Investigation
2. Conscientization
3. Admonishment
4. Motivation

We begin with the five questions proposed by Paul David Tripp. The investigation step encompasses the first of these; *What happened?* It is not enough merely to discover the trigger for the whole episode; a teacher needs to have a good understanding of the incident from beginning to end. Without this, she can hardly deal with the problem effectively. This step may require up to 60 or 70% of the entire counseling time. Listening intently to the child increases many-fold the probability that *he* will later listen to *your* counsel and accept whatever consequences might be forthcoming. Obviously, it requires good listening skills and intelligent information gathering by asking good questions.

During the investigation step, it is important to keep order. This can be particularly difficult when resolving issues between two children who have been fighting. Always, the Christian school teacher or counselor should maintain adherence to some basic parameters in order to have an effective information gathering time.

1. **Do not permit the children to speak to one another** in the information gathering phase. That often breeds accusations and responses which quickly get you nowhere. If the children are still at all angry one with another, make them each address *you* directly and exclusively.

2. **Never allow the children to interrupt each other**. Always let the offending child in this case know, in no uncertain terms, that he is not to interrupt his fellow even if he doesn't agree with something. Assure him that he will have his turn to talk in which his fellow will not be allowed to interrupt him either.

3. **Never allow a child to accuse another of lying**. First, it is offensive and never conducive to resolving a problem. Second, it is my experience that children may remember or interpret things in different ways, but they seldom lie when dealing with the details of a fight. If they do, it is the teacher's job to lead *them* to recognize it and not accuse.

4. **Don't get caught up into detail**. Often children interpret the same fact in very different ways. A good listener should not get caught up in whether Johnny pushed Jimmy as Johnny asserts, or Johnny hit Jimmy as Jimmy claims. From both testimonies, it is clear that Johnny aggressively struck Jimmy,

and whether it was a push or a blow is simply not worth debating.

5. **Ask who, what, where, when, and how**. Ask as many questions as are needed to understand as fully as the children are capable of telling it, exactly what happened.

6. **Repeat the child's testimony back to him to ensure you've got it right**. If you don't, have him repeat it until he agrees you've got it.

Once we have successfully navigated the investigation step, it is time to pass to conscientization step. What are his motivations for having done what he did? A principle of Biblical Counseling which my trainers from Faith church emphasized over and over is that as human beings, we do what we do because we want what we want, and we want what we want because we worship what we worship. This step is designed to expose to us and to the child himself the idols of his heart. It is important to realize, too, that not all idols are worshipped for love or passion. Some are worshipped out of fear. We have learned, as we have studied the effects of trauma on children, that bad behavior is the language of a child who has lost his voice. Of this statement, we must make two observations. First of all, it is not always true. A child without trauma is not the equivalent of a well-behaved child. Adam and Eve certainly had suffered no trauma in their lives that led to their sin. Some of our idols *are* worshipped due to love or passion. To give a practical illustration of what I am talking about here, a child may steal food because he has suffered the trauma of hunger in the past and fears being hungry again. On the other hand, he may steal something just because he wants it. These two stories represent the same act, but two very different idols. Second, that a child's fears render him incapable of overcoming sinful behavior does not diminish the fact that it *is* sinful behavior and should be dealt with as such. It may change the manner with which we deal with the sin, but we should deal with it as sin.

This is the step when we ask Paul Tripp's other four questions. *What were your thoughts and emotions when this happened?* Usually, this question speaks of the initial provocation and refers to the emotions that drove him to react in a certain way. It does not speak of his emotions when the whole thing was over. *What did you do in response? Why did you do it? What were you trying to achieve?* Finally, *What were the results? Did you get what you really wanted?* Usually, the answer to this question is no. Why else would a fight break out? These or similar questions help a child understand his own actions which, in the case of an amygdala hijacking, is particularly important to walk through.

After this, we come to the third stage, that of admonishing. This is the step where we ask the question, *What did you do wrong?* and walk a child through the repentance process, restoring his relationships with God, his teachers, and his fellow students.

The fourth and last stage is the motivation stage. While I call this the fourth stage, depending on the circumstances, it doesn't necessarily always follow strictly in order after the admonishing stage. It may often precede it. It is in this stage that we introduce the Bible.

Applying the Scriptures

It is important to remember the proper use of the Scriptures before we speak of applying them. As we saw in the last chapter from Hebrews 4:12-13, the Scriptures should be used as a surgical knife and not as a hammer. This is the stage in which we will attempt to do spiritual surgery to treat the cancerous sin within the child. Further suggestions for the application of the Scriptures are as follow:

1. Whenever the child's academic development is advanced enough, let *him* read the text. It is always good to place the Word of God into the child's own hands and let him navigate it for himself.

2. For long passages, give the child a summary of the story, and then have him read only the verses that you particularly wish to highlight. Otherwise, it may be easy to get bogged down in details otherwise irrelevant to the situation.

3. Ask the child what the scripture means and how it applies to his situation. The more he is encouraged to think and interpret for himself, the more effective the instruction will be.

4. Put on your didaskalos hat, and teach your application if the child is unable to see it for himself.

5. Be brief and speak as little as possible. In that sense, try to transcend your didaskalos hat. You are more likely to lose, than to win prizes for your natural teacher's verbosity.

6. Sometimes, it may be necessary to address the idols in the child's heart before actually addressing the behavior itself. In this case a simple presentation of the gospel may be in order. It may take a trip beyond earthly boundaries to the heavenly realm to tear down those idols in his heart. This means giving a simple presentation of the gospel tailored particularly to the idol which he needs to overcome.

A Tool Bag of Practical Passages

We shall spend the rest of this chapter presenting a number of scriptures to apply to common disciplinary challenges within the classroom. A truly Christian teacher should develop the habit of filling her own scriptural tool box for herself, but to get you started, I would like to present 14 different passages or verses I have found useful.

1. Daniel 1:8-21 This is the story of Daniel and the King's food which we discussed at some length in the last chapter. I will not repeat what I said there.

2. Proverbs 15:1 *A gentle answer turns away wrath But a harsh word stirs up anger.* This verse I also discussed in the last chapter.

3. Mark 9:33-37 We discussed this passage in chapter 4 as an example of turning a disciplinary situation into a teachable moment. However, it speaks to children as well. As the disciples heatedly argue about which of them would be

greatest in the Kingdom, so children often jockey for status within the classroom. This pride manifests itself in a child in a number of ways, such as fighting for the best seat or for the first spot in line, such as by displaying his intelligence in answering every question the teacher gives to the class, or such as by insisting upon "telling on" his fellow students for every minor infraction of the rules. Verse 35 says: *If anyone wants to be first, he shall be last of all and servant of all.* (It would probably not do much good to cite the part about becoming like little children. That may have worked for Jesus' disciples, but probably not for those who are already little children.) *Do you really want to be first?* we might ask them. It isn't a bad thing to want to be first, but if you want to be first in God's eyes, you should count other people first in the way you treat them.

4. Ephesians 6:12 *For our struggle is not against flesh and blood, but against the rulers, against the powers, against the world forces of this darkness, against the spiritual forces of wickedness in the heavenly places.* When two children are having difficulty getting along, I like to tell them of an episode of the old Star Trek series where an alien being made of energy came on board the Enterprise and orchestrated the escape of some Klingon prisoners and a subsequent battle between them and the crew. It provided swords and lances and miraculous healing for each injured person. The alien literally fed off of the energy of the hatred that it generated and thus grew stronger and stronger. When Captain Kirk and his crew finally discovered the alien presence with the ship's sensors, they ended their fight with the Klingons. Finding its food source exhausted, the alien was forced to flee the ship and look elsewhere for its sustenance. This is a vivid illustration of Ephesians 6:12. The devil is an alien being feeding off our anger and hatred toward others. He is the only one who truly wins our fights. For younger kids who are not familiar with Star Trek, I just retell the story naming the alien, the anger eater. It is a fun way to explain to them that when they fight, only the devil is happy.

5. Genesis 25:29-34 Esau sells his birthright. This story is short, and while one might be tempted to just tell it, it is always good to get out the Bible and read it. As I also explained in chapter 2, this is a story to help a child overcome spiritual near-sightedness. Thus, we try to divert a child's eyes away from the things that he sees, and focus them on the greater birthright related things he cannot see. This teaching may be applied to a variety of classroom issues. After all, no one ever sins when truly meditating on eternity.

6. Luke 10:25-37 The Parable of the Good Samaritan may be applied any time a child is showing a marked lack of compassion for his fellows. It may be particularly applied to children who pile on the bandwagon with bullies, thus making the bully's victim feel literally all alone in the world.

7. Matthew 7:12 The Golden Rule *In everything therefore treat people the same way you want them to treat you, for this is the Law and the Prophets.* This verse may be, again, applied to any offense a child commits against his fellow. It is particularly effective for small children for whom it is easy to learn and easy to understand.

8. 1 Samuel 25 The Story of David and Abigail This is probably not one of the better-known stories of the Bible, but the way in which Abigail pacifies David's righteous anger is a case study in prudence. David's men had been protecting the livestock of a wealthy man named Nabal, and after some time, David sent his men to ask for some sort of payment. Now, we might feel that David was a little forward here, but it is clear from the actions of Nabal's own servants that, culturally, there was no question but that David had every right to ask for this thing. Nabal not only refuses the request, but insults David's ambassadors. David commands his men to buckle on their armor and swears that there will not be a man left to Nabal before another night had gone by. Having heard of her husband's insults, Abigail quickly prepares gifts for David and his men and personally rides out to meet him, bowing low before him. An older child will benefit greatly from studying

Abigail's response to David and probably come up with ways to apply Abigail's wisdom to his own situation that even his teacher would not come up with. Abigail's rather lengthy response to David is expressed in verses 23-31. *When Abigail saw David, she hurried and dismounted from her donkey and fell on her face in front of David and bowed herself to the ground. 24 She fell at his feet and said, "On me alone, my lord, be the blame. And please let your slave speak to you and listen to the words of your slave. 25 Please, do not let my lord pay attention to this worthless man, Nabal, for as his name is so is he. Nabal is his name and stupidity is with him; but I, your slave, did not see the young men of my lord whom you sent. 26 "Now then, my lord, as the LORD lives and as your soul lives, since the LORD has restrained you from shedding blood and from avenging yourself by your own hand, now then may your enemies and those who seek evil against my lord be like Nabal. 27 And now let this gift which your servant has brought to my lord be given to the young men who accompany my lord. 28 Please, forgive the offense of your slave; for the LORD will certainly make for my lord an enduring house because my lord is fighting the battles of the LORD and evil will not be found in you all your days. 29 Should anyone rise up to pursue you and to seek your life, then the life of my lord shall be bound in the bundle of the living with the LORD your God; but the lives of your enemies, He will sling out as from the hollow of a sling. 30 And when the LORD does for my lord in accordance with all the good that He has spoken concerning you and appoints you ruler over Israel, 31 this will not become an obstacle to you or a troubled heart to my lord both by having shed blood without cause and by my lord's having avenged himself. When the LORD deals well with my lord, then remember your slave."*

9. 2 Samuel 6:14-23 David dances before the Lord. In this story, David brings back the Ark to Jerusalem, and in the joy of celebration, he dances with wild abandon before the Lord. When he returns home to bless his household, his wife Michal sarcastically berates him in verses 20-22: *"How the king of Israel dignified himself today! For he exposed himself today in the sight of his servants' female slaves as one of the rabble*

shamelessly exposes himself!" [21] But David said to Michal, "I was before the LORD *who preferred me to your father and to all his house to appoint me as ruler over the people of the* LORD *over Israel. So, I will celebrate before the* LORD*! [22] And I might demean myself even more than this and be lowly in my own sight, but with the female slaves of whom you have spoken, with them I am to be held in honor!"* Children should be more concerned with what God thinks of them than what people think in situations where they may have been treated contemptuously by their fellows.

10. Galatians 6:7 *Do not be deceived, God is not mocked; for whatever a person sows, this he will also reap.* This is another verse that may be applied in a variety of circumstances to make a kid realize that actions have consequences, and if he makes bad decisions, he can expect negative consequences.

11. Proverbs 19:24 and 22:13 are humorous verses that speak to the lazy student in a tongue-in-cheek manner. Verse 19:24 says: *The lazy one buries his hand in the dish, But will not even bring it back to his mouth.* Verse 22:13 says: *The lazy one says "There is a lion outside; I will be killed in the streets!"*

12. Mark 7:24-30 The prudence of the Syrophoenician woman. This story is fascinating. *Now Jesus got up and went from there to the region of Tyre. And when He had entered a house, He wanted no one to know about it; and yet He could not escape notice. [25]But after hearing about Him, a woman whose little daughter had an unclean spirit immediately came and fell at His feet. [26]Now the woman was a Gentile of Syrophoenician descent. And she repeatedly asked Him to cast the demon out of her daughter.[27]And He was saying to her, "Let the children be satisfied first, for it is not good to take the children's bread and throw it to the dogs."[28]But she answered and said to Him "Yes Lord, but even the dogs under the table feed on the children's crumbs." [29]And He said to her, "Because of this answer go; the demon has gone out of your daughter." [30]And after going back to her home, she found the child lying on the*

bed and the demon gone. Jesus called this woman a dog. Now we can be sure that, in some way or another, Jesus' words had a deeper design than to insult her, but it can hardly be denied that one might easily have taken offense at His words. This woman answered Jesus very prudently as our children might also learn to do in the face of insults which are much more intentional.

13. Proverbs 16:28, 26:10 speak of those who are anxious to tell tales. Verse 16:28 says: *A perverse person spreads strife, And a slanderer separates close friends.* Verse 26:10 says: *Like charcoal to hot embers and wood to fire, So is a contentious person to kindle strife.* Many fights I have seen provoked because one child went and told another something about one of his fellows that he had no business relating. This little slanderer often stirs up the flames and enjoys the spectacle of a good fight and gets off scot free as the combatants get all the attention from their teachers. Invariably the combatants have believed their friend who, as likely as not, was telling, intentionally or unintentionally, at best a half truth. We should not let a matter like this end without dealing with this little story teller.

14. Luke 12:2-3 *But there is nothing covered up that will not be revealed and hidden that will not be known. ³ Accordingly, whatever you have said in the dark will be heard in the light, and what you have whispered in the inner rooms will be proclaimed on the housetops.* This is a hard truth for young liars. Most children lie to cover up their own misdeeds. Here is a passage that will speak to them clearly of the futility of untruths.

Reflection If you are going through this book in a group, I encourage you to do a little role playing on a couple of these Scriptures as they may be applied in some kind of disciplinary situation. Also think of other situations that you have faced in your classroom and other scriptures you might add to your tool box. Write down your thoughts.

VIII. When it's the Teacher's Fault

Teacher's Problem, Teacher's Responsibility

We counselors are truly mighty people! (A little bit of exaggeration here.) We can work problems of fights or arguments between children. We can work issues regarding cheating or stealing or sexual difficulties. Counselors can work many, many issues, but our power has its limits. We cannot work situations where the teacher shares in the responsibility for the problem. As a counselor, I did not realize this for years and always tried to work out such problems with just the student. Needless to say, my results were somewhat less than stellar. When teachers share in responsibility for the problem, they must share in the solution as well.

Now having said this, I must make a couple clarifications. First of all, that a counselor may not *resolve* a problem does not mean that he may not act as a facilitator, but it does mean that he cannot do it by himself. Secondly, it may be that the teacher's fault was in poor lesson planning or supervision. In this case, her share in the problem is indirect and the counselor may embark on a successful resolution without her help, though she would do well to avoid such errors in the future. However, when a relationship problem is manifested between the teacher and a student, the teacher *must* participate if a real and lasting solution is to be achieved. Now, the teacher might often not realize her responsibility. The student may have misinterpreted something she said or did and need to hear a clarification that only she can give him. In this case, the counselor must rightly discern the situation and seek her participation.

The Infallibility Myth

What is the difference between the pope and a teacher? Give up? The pope is only infallible when he is speaking ex cathedra. A teacher *never* errs when standing in front of her students. At least we act as if we believe that most of the time.

It is time for a thorough study of the James 3 discourse on the tongue. Let us break it down a verse or two at a time:

> **Do not become teachers in large numbers, my brothers, since you know that we who are teachers will incur a stricter judgment. [2] For we all stumble in many ways. If anyone does not stumble in what he says, he is a perfect man, able to rein in the whole body as well.**

Here James warns us plainly against becoming teachers without the necessary competence, calling, or even spiritual maturity. The reason is that all who have the ability to speak, err in what we say, and teaching requires the constant use of the tongue. When others may be permitted to remain in silence, a teacher has no choice but to speak. As I have told students many times, they always have the option of keeping their mouths shut, but a teacher, who is responsible for discipline within the classroom, does not have the option to overlook or ignore certain behaviors. She must speak to these, and the authority exercised by a teacher will bring over her a stricter judgment. Teaching, then, is a profession that should not be entered into heedlessly.

> **[3] Now if we put the bits into the horses' mouths so that they will obey us, we direct their whole body as well. [4] Look at the ships too: though they are so large and are driven by strong winds, they are, nevertheless, directed by a very small rudder wherever the inclination of the pilot determines. [5] So also the tongue is a small part of the body, and yet it boasts of great things.**

Now we would think that our bodies must govern our tongues, but as these two verses express so eloquently, in life the tongue itself often controls the very direction of our lives. How often do we speak rashly or make a foolish promise or a statement that we then cannot withdraw? Like the old Law of the Medes and the Persians that bound kings to their decrees even when those decrees had unintended consequences (such as when Darius was forced to cast Daniel into the Lion's den), we must adjust the entire direction of our lives in order to compensate for the words we have uttered. A biblical example is King Herod in Matthew 14 when he rashly made a promise to his step-daughter to give her anything she desired. His words obligated him to kill John the Baptist or suffer a rather radical change in diet and the good king was not fond of crow. Another is Jephthah's rash promise to sacrifice as a burnt offering the first one who came out to greet him on his return home from battle. His only beloved daughter turned out to be the victim. Now this story is inconsistent with the rest of the Scriptures in that God never condones human sacrifice, so this passage may not carry the normal meaning of that term, but it is clear that whatever it meant, Jephthah, seeing the results, very much regretted his vow. Thus, Herod's words and Jephthah's moved their lives in a direction that they never desired, but were helpless afterward to change. In the same way, a teacher's words could also bind her to a course she afterwards may not have wished. I recall one time when, in our own school, we made a decision to expel a certain child, but later circumstances arose which led us, in many ways, to regret that decision. Nevertheless, the administration felt bound by its words to proceed with our original plan despite the inconveniences it caused.

> **See how great a forest is set aflame by such a small fire! [6]And the tongue is a fire, the very world of unrighteousness; the tongue is set among our body's parts as that which defiles the whole body and sets on fire the course of our life and is set on fire by hell.**

The second law of thermodynamics tells us that all things move toward disorder. The tongue serves as a vibrant affirmation of this law even outside the realm of physics. Just as an earthquake will destroy, rather than build, the tongue, unbridled in a moment of amygdala hijacking, will destroy, rather than edify, turning our entire lives towards all its indiscretions. Lies beget more lies. Calumny begets more calumny. Angry words beget more angry words setting fire to previously nurturing relationships. Thus, the tongue represents a prime target for every satanic enterprise. Proverbs 18:21 tells us that: *Death and life are in the power of the tongue,* and 10:11 says: *The mouth of the righteous is a fountain of life, But the mouth of the wicked conceals violence.*

> **⁷ For every species of beasts and birds, of reptiles and creatures of the sea is tamed and has been tamed by the human race. ⁸ But no one among mankind can tame the tongue; it is a restless evil full of deadly poison.**

Without a doubt, James is making rich use of exaggeration here, but his point couldn't be clearer. Each one of us has, in our tongues, an acute power of destruction. It is as if we each move through life with a cocked pistol permanently affixed to our hands. Sooner or later, we will inadvertently fire it. It is too easy to pull! The tongue's hairspring trigger will fire at the slightest provocation, and each time that it starts, it is difficult to restrain it. Human beings may indeed make great strides toward taming the tongue, but we can never fully manage it. These are the dangers that we face as teachers who make careers of our tongues.

> **⁹ With it we bless our Lord and Father, and with it we curse people who have been made in the likeness of God; ¹⁰from the same mouth come both blessing and cursing. My brothers and sisters, these things should not be this way.**

What more can one say?

> **¹¹ Does a spring send out from the same opening both fresh and bitter water? ¹² Can a fig tree, my brothers and sisters, bear olives or a vine bear figs? Nor can salt water produce fresh.**

Proverbs 10:19 tells us: *When there are many words, wrongdoing is unavoidable, But one who restrains his lips is wise.* And 29:20 says: *Do you see a person who is hasty with his words? There is more hope for a fool than for him.* Surely a teacher, of whom is demanded nearly constant use of the tongue, is ripe for a fall. We judiciously plan our prayers and praises, but when we teach, the mind does not often plan its insults. These flow freely and naturally.

Now, while we may not have expressed ourselves in such strong language as James in his place, we know what he says to be true. Despite the façade we are so hesitant to drop, we know very well, as teachers, our capacity and propensity to fall. And yet the fear of looking weak before our students is constantly before us, keeping us from doing what we know to be right, humbly confessing before them our weakness and sinfulness. We do not serve the public schools nor earthly authorities, and we should not act as public-school teachers. We serve our Lord and Savior, Jesus Christ. Let us remember the words of Proverbs: 25:15, that it is, *Through patience, a ruler may be persuaded, And a gentle tongue breaks bone.* If a ruler be thus persuaded, how much more a child. Let us also remember the command of Proverbs 27:2 to *Let another praise you and not your own mouth; A stranger and not your own lips.* A stranger? How about our students?

Becoming the Living Gospel

Never try to model Christ in front of your students! There is a big difference between you and Christ; He was perfect, and you are not. We need to become a living gospel for our students a living, breathing testimony of the power of Jesus Christ to transform lives. In truth, the life, crucifixion, and resurrection of Jesus Christ are not the gospel. The gospel is how these things have worked in me. We must strive to live before our students so that they might see our good works and glorify our Father in heaven!

How do we do this? First, let us take deadly seriously the truths of whom we are dealing with as we work with children:

> **And whoever receives one such child in My name receives Me; [6]but whoever causes one of these little ones who believe in Me to sin, it is better for him that a heavy millstone be hung around his neck and that he be drowned in the depths of the sea. (Matthew 18:5-6)**

> **"See that you do not look down on one of these little ones; for I say to you that their angels in heaven continually see the face of My Father who is in heaven. (Matthew 18:10)**

Given these sobering words, should we not also apply Matthew 5:23-24 to our work as teachers?

> **Therefore, if you are presenting your offering at the altar and there you remember that your brother has something against you, [24] leave your offering there before the altar and go; first be reconciled to your brother, and then come and present your offering.**

And this verse reminds us of Malachi 2:13-14:

> **And this is another thing you do: you cover the altar of the LORD with tears, with weeping, and sighing because He no longer gives attention to the offering or accepts it with favor from your hand. [14] Yet you say, "For what reason?"**

The answer the text gives to this question is that it is for their infidelity toward their wives that God does not accept their offerings, but does not the text in Matthew 5 seem to indicate that our relationships with others beyond our spouses might also affect our relationship with the Lord and His acceptance of our offerings? Certainly, work with children must be undertaken with all diligence and discipline.

> **Therefore, I run in such a way as not to run aimlessly; I box in such a way as to avoid hitting air; [27] but I strictly discipline my body and make it my slave so that after I have preached to others, I myself will not be disqualified. (1 Corinthians 9:26-27)**

Let us remember also the words of Jesus to his disciples:

> **But Jesus called them to Himself and said, "You know that the rulers of the Gentiles domineer over them, and those in high position exercise authority over them. [26] It is not this way among you, but whoever wants to become prominent among you shall be your servant." (Matthew 20:25-26)**

Should we not apply these words to our work as teachers and counselors in Christian schools? The teachers of secular schools domineer over them, and those in high position exercise authority over them. It is not this way among you teachers of Christian schools, but whoever wants to become prominent among you shall be their servant. Should we not be servants to our students? James 4:10 tells us: *Humble yourselves in the presence of the Lord, and He will exalt you.*

What better place to do that than in the classroom in front of our students!

In brief, it is incumbent upon the Christian teacher to do everything possible to maintain a healthy relationship with her students, and in order to do that, she must recognize her ability—no rather her propensity—to offend those little ones who sit under her teaching. She must always be quick to attend to the feelings of her students and ask the problem when she perceives she might have offended. If and when it is possible, she must be ready to ask forgiveness of her students, even if the offense was unintentional and promise to take into account their feelings in the future.

Reflection In what way may you have offended your students in the past? What situations do you have right now in your classroom that may require attention? Have you noticed how any problems you may have in relationship with some student have affected your relationship with God? What ought you do?

IX. Breaking Patterns: Plan B for Bible

In the very first chapter of this book, we divided the issue of discipline into three parts: the proactive, the reactive, and the reactive-proactive. We stated that the proactive element of discipline involves everything we do in our schools that isn't part of the other two, including lesson planning, classroom organization, and even such things as food programs designed to keep kids comfortable and thereby give them the best opportunity to behave well. Throughout the first eight chapters of this book, we have then spoken of the reactive portion of discipline where an actual problem surfaces, and we must respond to it. In this chapter, we will speak of the third area of discipline, the reactive-proactive portion—that is, learning from past problems to work to prevent future ones. Since we have identified the primary purpose of discipline in a Christian school as the salvation and sanctification of our students, it is not my habit to search for wisdom in achieving those goals from secular sources. However, I have become familiar with one particular source that does offer some helpful suggestions, and although we must develop a plan fully conformed to the Word of God, I must, at the same time, give credit where credit is due. Pedopsychologist Dr. Ross Greene is founder of *Lives in the Balance* and *Collaborative and Interactive Solutions.* He has developed a structure for this reactive-proactive portion of classroom discipline which he calls Plan B. While Plan B has many weaknesses inherent to any secular discipline plan, it does have a number of facets consistent with the Word of God which we shall use to develop a biblically centered plan of our own. Without further adieu then, I shall first give a brief introduction to Plan B and then extract those principles which are of use to us in developing our own plan.

Plan B

Dr. Greene's basic premise is that Plan A, our traditional teacher-centered, reward-punishment philosophy of classroom discipline, simply has not worked, and that many children have fallen through the cracks in our public-school systems. He begins with the postulate that every child will do well if he can because to do well is always preferable, and if a child is not doing well, it is because of some likely impediment over which he has no control. Greene's solution is to enlist the children themselves as partners in resolving disciplinary problems. Through constructive conversations, it is hoped that these impediments shall be revealed and solutions developed to compensate for them in which the child himself shall be thoroughly invested.

Dr. Greene actually describes three different disciplinary approaches as follows:

- Plan A   The traditional teacher-centered reward-punishment problem solving strategy.

- Plan B   The new collaborative strategy where both teacher and student concerns are addressed.

- Plan C   A strategic setting aside of a problem until a more propitious moment.

The first problem with the traditional Plan A is that it imposes a solution upon the student in which he has no particular investment. Secondly, Plan A is reactionary. Consequences follow behaviors. Thirdly, it does not resolve and rarely even discovers the underlying problem behind the bad behavior. For instance, a poor grade on a homework does not resolve the problem that kept the student from completing the assignment in the first place.

Plan B consists of three steps. During the empathy step, the child is encouraged to express his concerns, hopefully revealing what makes it difficult for him to behave properly. Then, we define the teacher's concern. Finally, we have the invitation to propose a solution designed to resolve both the child's and the teacher's concerns.

The empathy step is certainly the most complex of the three as it depends largely on the child's willingness to cooperate with the teacher and on the teacher's ability to interpret what the child says. Its purpose is, first of all, to gain the child's trust. The teacher must work to successfully convince the child that she is interested in working with him to resolve the problem and is not merely seeking another opportunity to punish or condemn him. Secondly, the purpose is to gather information in order to understand the underlying impediments to a child's capacity to fulfill classroom expectations. The teacher should initiate the conversation with a non-condemning explanation of the unresolved problem beginning with *I've noticed that....* Then the child's participation will be invited with the question, *What's up?*

If the child answers, the conversation may move forward. However, a child accustomed to teacher-imposed Plan-A solutions may respond defensively with answers such as, *I don't have to tell you.* He may respond with the evasive, *I don't know,* or he may deny having the problem at all. He may simply express that he does not want to talk about the matter. The teacher may strive to set the child at ease by asking how he feels and looking for a more descriptive answer than *bad.* She may follow up by asking him *why* he feels that way. Otherwise, the teacher may ask the child why he doesn't wish to respond. Sometimes, the child may simply not know how to express his feelings. On such occasions, the teacher may make speculations to which the child may simply respond with a simple yes or no. If the child seems to expect some form of punishment, the teacher must assure him that the purpose of the meeting is, on the contrary, to help him avoid getting in trouble. If the teacher perceives that her relationship with the child is strained, she may seek another member of the staff as an intermediary who has a better repour with the student.

Once the child is engaged follow-up questions are very important. First, we need to understand the who what where and when of the child's difficulties. Does he have difficulty with particular people or things? Is there a particular circumstance or time in which he has difficulty? Second the teacher should ask what the child is thinking when the difficulty arises. Does this question sound familiar? (Paul Tripp chapter 6) Sometimes, it is helpful to break up a complex problem into its component parts. Perhaps the child does not understand himself the reasons for his difficulties. Therefore, we must note and ask about any apparent contradictions in the information he gives. Finally, it is often necessary to concentrate on certain aspects of the problem and leave other aspects to one side for the moment.

After the empathy step we come to the presentation of the teacher's concern. This step may be engaged with the phrase *The thing is...* or perhaps *My concern is...* The teacher's concern is not simply a repetition of the expectation that the child is not meeting. Her concern will have to do with how that violation of the expectation is affecting the child himself and the other people around him. These concerns generally speak to the health safety or learning of the child or his companions.

Finally, we come to the invitation step. The goal of this step is to collaborate with the student to come to a mutually satisfactory solution which addresses both the student and the teacher concerns. It is introduced by first recapitulating those concerns and verifying that the student is in agreement with them. Then the invitation is given beginning with a statement resembling the following: *I wonder if there is a way in which we could work together to solve both our problems. Do you have any ideas?* The child is accustomed to having the solutions to his discipline problems handed to him, so to help him understand that you truly welcome his participation this time, it is essential that he be given the first opportunity to propose a solution. Quite likely, his initial proposal will solve only his concern and not the teacher's. In this case, he simply must be reminded, *That sounds like it would solve your problem pretty well but I don't think it would solve mine do you think?* The teacher may propose a solution if the child is unable to think of one, but as the child's solution must resolve the teacher's concern as well as his own, so must the child be satisfied that the teacher's solution satisfies *his* concern.

Plan B Rollout, Little by Little

Sometimes a child has multiple problems with multiple teachers. In cases like this, it is important to form a strategy to work through his difficulties one by one. All the affected teachers must get together to form a plan of attack. To help develop such a plan, Dr. Greene has provided a worksheet called the Assessment of Lagging Skills and Unsolved Problems or ALSUP.

The ALSUP is a list of twenty-four typical skills which typical problem children might well be lacking. It begins with such things as *difficulty handling transitions, difficulty doing things in a logical sequence or prescribed order, and difficulty persisting on challenging or tedious tasks.*

However, the ALSUP is not an end in and of itself. While it may be helpful to understand the lagging skills, we must not get hung up on them. The goal is to identify the unsolved problems that these lagging skills cause for the teacher and the student himself. As the team works through the list for a particular student, every time a lagging skill is identified, beside that skill the team should list the problem or problems that lagging skill causes. It is these problems, we are to work through. For example, a difficulty handling transitions may mean that a child never wishes to put his books for math class away and get out his English books. It may mean that he simply loses focus and wants to get out of his seat and run around at the start of the new class period. It may mean any number of specific problems at specific times of the day. Each of these problems should be recorded next to this lagging skill.

After having worked through the ALSUP and successfully identified each unsolved problem, the team chooses two or three on which to focus. These should be prioritized based on safety issues, frequency, and general degree of seriousness. Other problems are relegated to Plan C until the priority problems are resolved. After this, a teacher should be chosen to schedule a follow up Plan B meeting with the student to tackle the problems identified. The teacher chosen should be the one primarily affected by those problems. Progress should be celebrated.

Before we move on to develop our Plan B for Bible, I would like to make one philosophically critical comment at this point. While I present the use of the ALSUP here, I really see very little value in it. First of all, Dr. Greene's list is so cumbersome that I often have to read many of those possible lagging skills several times before I can begin to make heads or tails of them. For instance, we have the lagging skill identified as *difficulty doing things in a logical sequence or prescribed order.* What does that even look like in real life? I'm not sure I've ever met a child who had this problem although probably

I just did not recognize it when I saw it. Further, Dr. Greene himself tells us that the end goal is to establish a list of unresolved problems and identifying these lagging skills is meant only to aid us on our way. My question then is, what good are they? If we didn't already have a good idea as to what a child's unresolved problems are we probably wouldn't have called the meeting in the first place.

The Philosophical Origin of Plan B

Plan B, along with so many other secular plans, came to light as a reaction against what began as a biblically based discipline plan. The Plan A concept of punishment for wrong-doing is, in every way, consistent with biblical teaching as we have laid it out in this book. Our very system of education itself has been based for long centuries past upon our Christian heritage. Every institution of higher learning in the West that has existed for more than a century was, nearly without exception, founded as a Christian university. Likewise, our lower education was also founded upon biblical principles in its origins in the distant past. Our Plan A system of discipline itself is very much based upon the concept of the tutorial law as laid out in the Bible and as we shall develop further in the next chapter. We have argued in chapter 5 that the school's discipline is developed as an extension of parental authority, and thus, throughout our long history, have educators seen it. The problem with the traditional Plan A is not that it is wrong, but that it is incomplete. It speaks of the consequences of the law without the foundation of grace. As our Christian institutions have become subjected to the legalistic Calvinism of the past and more recently have become increasingly more secularized, the concept of grace has disappeared leaving only the law behind, and this has produced the bitter fruit against which Dr. Greene and others have waged their war. They have reacted in antagonism against the law and have attempted to replace it with their secular form of grace as represented by Plan B. In reality, the two should walk hand in hand. In our plan they shall do so, as we have already shown in chapter 5.

The Value of Plan B

So, in the end, just what does Plan B have to teach us? It is, as I have said, a form of grace, and within it are some very biblically-based elements that should certainly be part of our Plan B for Bible. Just what are they?

First of all, it suggests to us that a child may be incapable of overcoming a particular sin in his life. Now, we do not accept the universal application of Dr. Greene's basic premise that a child will do well if he can. This concept denies the reality of sin which is at the core of biblical understanding. We are naturally rebellious creatures and may well fail simply because we do not have the desire to succeed. However, in any given case, Dr. Green may be right. Unlike the secularists, we shall call sin, sin, but just because something is a sin does not mean that an individual can overcome it by himself. Rather than continually punishing a child for a repeated sin, we shall acknowledge the possibility that he does *not* have within himself the power to overcome it and that if offered assistance, he may be willing to try.

Second, Dr. Greene exalts the attitude of listening to the child and asking probing questions to draw him out as we also have done throughout this book. We recall the words of Proverbs 20:5: *A plan in the heart of a man is like deep water, But a man of understanding draws it out,* and strive to be that man or woman of understanding that draws out of the child what he does not know how nor, in some cases, wish to express.

Third, even if Dr. Greene does not use the word, his method gives a child a voice and empowers him to take an active part in resolving and overcoming his own sin. Plan B becomes, for the teacher, a time of parakaleo, collaboratively motivating and encouraging him to action against the evil within him rather than sitting back and passively accepting it. It represents an opportunity for the teacher to work together with the child to mold his character, empowering him to meet issues in his own life head on and find solutions.

Plan B for Bible

Plan B for Bible begins and ends with the Word of our God which gives us a huge advantage over any secular school. As Christian educators, we never forget that *All Scripture is inspired by God and profitable for teaching, for reproof, for correction, for training in righteousness; so that the man of God may be adequate equipped for every good work* (2 Timothy 3:16-17) nor that: *the word of God is living and active and sharper than any two-edged sword even penetrating as far as the division of soul and spirit of both joints and marrow and able to judge the thoughts and intentions of the heart.* (Hebrews 4:12)

Plan B for Bible recognizes and deals with sin, head on. As we have said, this simple foundational belief that we are all constant violators of all that we recognize as good, empowers a child because it takes away the victim mentality and places solutions within his grasp. After all, he may have no control over what others do to him, but he does have control over himself, and with a paracletic teacher armed with the Word of God there to support him, he is empowered to make life adjustments to resolve his own problems. We are not merely making our classroom a safer and more pleasant place and creating in it a more effective learning environment; we are helping a child grow into a man or woman of God.

A Plan B for Bible meeting always, always, begins with a word of prayer in which the child should be invited to participate. Then, as the empathy step begins, making a correct diagnosis of the child's problem is central. Is his sin really one to which he is enslaved and cannot escape without help? Are there factors that he cannot control that provoke his behavior? Have you, as his teacher, contributed to the child's problem, albeit unknowingly? Remember Matthew 23:12: *Whoever exalts himself shall be humbled, and whoever humbles himself shall be exalted.* It may often be necessary for the teacher to ask the child's forgiveness and or make significant adjustments in her own behavior. Is he simply rebellious? A great majority of the time if a child sees his teacher as on his side, he will desire to work with her but not always. Are there, perhaps, situations in his life outside the school that are affecting his behavior during the school day? Dr. Greene assumes that for such factors there is little a teacher can do and therefore makes very little effort to investigate them, but we do not make that assumption. As Christian educators we do everything we can to impact the entire home, offering counseling and sometimes even financial aid wherever God gives us the capacity and opportunity. We may not be able to resolve all problems that happen in the students' homes, but we have a powerful God who can and He often gives us wisdom that may be successfully applied in some very difficult situations. We do not fear to intervene when and if we can.

It may be that the child will wish to ask forgiveness for his behavior during the Plan B for Bible process. If this happens, then it is a welcome development, and we should handle it properly. An attitude change can be a game changer for poor classroom behavior. However, it is not the focus of Plan B and not what we are looking for. It is to be assumed that the issue of sin has been dealt with on previous occasions before we engage in a Plan B meeting. A Plan B for Bible meeting may resemble in some ways the meetings we would hold immediately after a disciplinary situation but the goals are now different. After a disciplinary situation the primary motives are to seek repentance and restore relationships. In Plan B for Bible meetings, we are digging deeper and attempting to find solutions for what have proven to be more complicated problems and help a child eliminate that sin from his life.

In the end then, we value and put to use the structure that Dr. Greene has given us, but our focus is far broader and our goals far higher than his. Plan B for Bible brings sin into the forefront, seeking to enlist the student to actively combat it, leading him ever forward in his spiritual journey toward Christ.

Reflection: Have you been, up to this point, more of a Plan A or a Plan B kind of teacher. In what occasions have you used a traditional Plan A to work through a given disciplinary situation? Did it work? If it did work, do you feel there was any real heart change in the child? Record all your thoughts.

X. Liberation Day

Our discussion of practical discipleship as it relates to disciplinary practice is at an end, but something is left to be said. After all, if the whole purpose of discipline is to lead a child to Christ and to disciple him afterwards, then it is worth our while to spend a chapter on how to get to that final result, or perhaps it would be better to call it that initial result, that is, how to win a child to Christ. A simple discipline plan will never be enough to win anyone to Christ although it can offer many opportunities for evangelistic conversations. Still, in the end, leading a child to Christ is fully an act of didaskalo.

We have many misconceptions and misinterpretations as to how to lead a child to Christ. These come because of a generational misunderstanding of what is really involved in being saved. In this chapter I hope to expose these misconceptions and identify the real needs that our children have in understanding and fully receiving the gospel of Christ.

Do Children Need to be Converted?

Now the evangelical church has fully embraced the concept that every human being needs to be converted to Christ. However, the word and concept of conversion is barely a biblical word at all. In fact, on a search engine, the word *convert* or *conversion* appear in the Scriptures perhaps a dozen times, but in almost all it is in titles of sections composed in modern days by modern translators to introduce such stories as the conversion of Zacchaeus or Cornelius or Paul. The Greek word translated *to convert* is $\sigma\tau\rho\epsilon\phi o$ (strepho) which literally means *to turn* and is used some 21 times in the New Testament, but usually in the context of something like *and Jesus turned to him and said...* Only twice does it properly refer to a spiritual conversion. John 12:40 says:

> **He has blinded their eyes, and He has hardened their
> heart so that they will not see with their eyes and understand
> with their heart and be converted and *so* I will *not* heal them.**

But of much more interest is Matthew 18:3:

> **Truly, I say to you, unless you are converted and
> become like children, you will not enter the kingdom of
> heaven.**

Now first, we must recognize that both of these passages are most definitely referring to adults. But the second thing we note is that in Matthew 18:3 those adults are told they must convert to become like children. Now if adults must become like children, to what are children supposed to convert?

One may cite Jesus' statement to Nicodemus in John 3:3 that one must be born again. What might it mean to be born again, but to be converted? However, of all the people that Jesus ever evangelized, with only one did He ever use the expression *born again*. Would He have denied such an important doctrinal point to all others that he ministered to, including His twelve disciples? Furthermore, in all the writings of Paul, that apostle never mentions the need to be born again. Nor does any other biblical author other than John in his first epistle. What do the gospels and the entire New Testament cite over and over again as necessary to enter the Kingdom of God? We must believe. Plain and simple; we must believe.

Thus, the evangelical conversion craze is simply not biblical! All of us must believe, but the idea that every believer must have had a darkness to light, spiritual death to life, one day to another conversion experience simply is not scriptural. To be sure, there are those who *do* experience such conversions, and there are those who *need to* experience such conversions, but those of us who were raised in the faith since our earliest childhood, whose physical birth was followed very closely by our spiritual birth, many times have a completely different experience.

Simply put, for children raised in a Christian home or even a Christian school, salvation is more of a gradual growth process than a radical conversion. Those who expect conversions of children will often be deceived. That is not to say that it is wrong to lead a child through the prayer of faith, but the simple fact is, that when you ask a room full of children how many of them would like to receive Jesus as their Savior, nearly every hand will likely shoot up. And the same hands will shoot up again tomorrow if you ask them the same question. As Christian adults we should not adopt naivety in the guise of spirituality! Has anything major really happened in their hearts? Where will each of these children be ten and fifteen years down the road? Years ago, I used to lead a series of summer Bible clubs for children in poor churches all over town. At the end of every summer, Child Evangelism Fellowship, whose material we used, would always ask for a number of conversions. It was a question I hated to answer because, how could I have any idea what God had truly done in their young hearts? Likely not a *single* child experienced a "conversion" in all those clubs I ran over the years, but hopefully for many of them the clubs may have represented one small step on their paths to a saving faith. For such children, we may even say that, to a degree, discipleship occurs before they arrive at that fully saving faith, and we have already argued that children, particularly those raised in Christian homes and schools, are protected by a special grace until the day that they arrive there, or on the contrary, that they actively walk away.

> **but whoever causes one of these little ones who believe in Me to sin, it is better for him that a heavy millstone be hung around his neck and that he be drowned in the depths of the sea. (Matthew 18:6)**

> **For the unbelieving husband is sanctified through his wife, and the unbelieving wife is sanctified through her believing husband;** *for otherwise your children are unclean, but now they are holy.* **(1 Corinthians 7:14)**

> **that their angels in heaven continually see the face of My Father who is in heaven. (Matthew 18:10)**

Nearly every child in our school can answer and truly believes the basic facts of what Jesus Christ did for him on the cross although later in life he may reject or deny it.

All this, then, being the case, what exact needs do our children have, and how do we supply them?

The Three Spiritual Laws

I remember, in my youth, always seeing those little evangelistic pamphlets put out by Campus Crusade for Christ entitled *The Four Spiritual Laws*. I must confess that I never really read those pamphlets and couldn't tell you to this day what the four spiritual laws are, but I think I can tell you truly that biblically there are actually three spiritual laws which Paul speaks of over and over again in the book of Romans. He gives various names to each of these laws but they are very distinctly three in number. In an order that I consider logical, but not necessarily biblical these are:

1. The Law of Justice, called the Law of Sin and Death or just the Law of Sin in the book of Romans.

2. The Instructional or Tutorial Law as represented by the Law of Moses sometimes called the Law of God in Romans.

3. The Law of Grace, called the Law of Faith or the Law of the Spirit in Romans.

Now the word *law* appears 52 times in the book of Romans. The vast majority of the references speak of our second law, the Law of the Old Testament or the Law of Moses. However, the first law is introduced as a distinct law from the second in 7:22-23:

> **For I joyfully agree with the law of God in the inner person, ²³ but I see a different law in the parts of my body waging war against the law of my mind and making me a prisoner of the law of sin, the law which is in my body's parts.**

Now in this verse, the word law appears five times. The first mention is *the law of God* which he later refers to as *the law of my mind.* We understand this from context to refer to the Law of Moses of which Paul has been speaking extensively and of which he heartily approves in his mind. Then, he refers to a different law in the parts of his body which wages war against that other law making him *a prisoner of the law of sin.* With that statement he names that new law and verifies it by saying once again that *the law of sin* is that different law *which is in my body's parts.* This is our first law, the law of justice that universally condemns all as sinners.

Then in verse 25, Paul lays it out much more clearly:

> **So then, on the one hand, I myself with my mind am serving the law of God, but on the other with my flesh, the law of sin.**

The third of these laws is first introduced in 3:27:

> **Where then is boasting? It has been excluded. By what kind of law? Of works? No but by a law of faith.**

Then in 8:2, the apostle speaks of both the first and the third laws when he says:

> **For the law of the Spirit of life in Christ Jesus has set you free from the law of sin and of death.**

The second law which is commonly called *the* Law serves as a bridge between the other two. This is the law that teaches us what sin is. As Paul says in 7:7-9:

> **What shall we say then? Is the Law sin? Far from it! On the contrary, I would not have come to know sin except through the Law; for I would not have known about coveting if the Law had not said, "YOU SHALL NOT COVET." [8] But sin, taking an opportunity through the commandment, produced in me coveting of every kind; for apart from the Law, sin is dead. [9] I was once alive apart from the Law; but when the commandment came, sin came to life, and I died;**

Further, as we studied in chapter 4, Romans 2:12-16 shows us that all men are subject to that tutorial law in one way or another:

> **For all who have sinned without the Law will also perish without the Law, and all who have sinned under the Law will be judged by the Law; [13] for it is not the hearers of the Law who are just before God, but the doers of the Law will be justified. [14] For when Gentiles who do not have the Law do instinctively the things of the Law, these, not having the Law, are a law to themselves [15] in that they show the work**

of the Law written in their hearts, their conscience bearing witness and their thoughts alternately accusing or else defending them [16] on the day when, according to my gospel, God will judge the secrets of men through Christ Jesus.

The Law serves as a tutor as described in Galatians 4:1-7:

Now I say, as long as the heir is a child, he does not differ at all from a slave although he is owner of everything, [2]but he is under guardians and managers until the date set by the father. [3] So we too, when we were children, were held in bondage under the elementary principles of the world. [4] But when the fullness of the time came, God sent His Son, born of a woman, born under the Law [5] so that He might redeem those who were under the Law that we might receive the adoption as sons and daughters. [6] Because you are sons, God has sent the Spirit of His Son into our hearts, crying out, "Abba! Father!" [7] Therefore you are no longer a slave, but a son; and if a son, then an heir through God.

This passage speaks of the nation of Israel, but it is more generally applicable to all people. When we are young, we are all instructed by the law so as to learn right from wrong. This extends beyond the Law of Moses to the general tutorial law wielded by all authorities in our lives and of which our consciences heartily approve, telling us we deserve punishment when we do not do what is right. This law instructs us until such a time as we are formally adopted as sons and daughters. In the Jewish culture of biblical times, even natural sons reached a point in their adolescence where they were formally recognized by their Fathers. For us who do not share the substance of our heavenly Father as Jesus Christ did, that moment of adoption is all the more poignant. That is the point when we experience the true freedom as sons and heirs of our Father, though we have lived like slaves to the tutor in our childhood.

The need of our children is to cross that threshold from their childhood in the charge of the tutor of the law to their freedom in adulthood as sons and daughters of their heavenly Father. Very few children who have grown up in a Christian home or in a Christian school are ignorant of the fact that Christ died to save them from their sins. They are no longer subject to the first law, but they are still subject to the second, to the tutor. As many times as you tell them that they can add nothing to their salvation and that Christ did everything that was necessary to save them completely independently of what they might do, it simply doesn't register. Everything in our beings screams out against such a doctrine in which we are saved no matter what we do! For children still under the tutor, Christ died to make it possible for them to go to heaven, but they still must add something to it. They still must not cross certain lines in their behavior or their salvation simply isn't real.

The great problem with all this is that even if Jesus Christ provided 99.99% of what is necessary to get to heaven, I know that I am not reliable even to supply that remaining 0.01%. Thus, as long as it depends in the slightest upon me, my entire salvation is always in doubt and true liberation beyond my grasp. The need of our children is to come to the point where they are freed from that tutor that demands even the 0.01% and formally recognized by their true Father of grace who supplies the entire 100% with no residual left over. To evangelize a child from a Christian home or school is to free him from the tutor. This usually occurs after an individual has left the special protective grace of his childhood and in adolescence has begun to ask the tougher questions of life. Thus, we speak of evangelization, not so much of children, but of youth.

Spiritual Diagnosis

Years ago, I took a course developed by the late D. James Kennedy called *Evangelism Explosion* which endeavored to teach how to share the gospel. I'm sure that many people have been very successful using *Evangelism Explosion,* but I personally found the approach entirely too detailed and too one-size-fits-all. Still, it supplied me with one thing that I have used ever since. It was what he called his diagnostic questions, two questions which reveal the spiritual condition of the respondent and which serve as an excellent spring board to launch into a discussion of spiritual things. These questions are:

1. If you died today, would you go to heaven?

2. If you died today and stood before the throne of God and He asked, *why should I let you into heaven,* how would you answer Him?

Now the answer to the first question is a simple *yes, no,* or *I don't know.* Seldom will I child answer *no* to that first question, although a youth may well do so, but uncertainty *is* a factor in children and youth perhaps more the norm than the exception. We will come back to this fact presently.

The second question is obviously much more complex. When I took the course, two basic answers were presented, the right answer and the wrong, but I have learned that, among those instructed in the faith, there is a little more nuance in the range of possible answers than at first I perceived.

The typical unbeliever sets his hope on his own behavior, what we in the Christian community call *works.* This is expressed in a number of different forms. *I always try to get along with everyone; I go to church; I always try to do what is right. I read the Bible.* For anyone even slightly versed in the Scriptures, the problem with these answers is easily discerned and easily answered by Ephesians 2:8-9 which we shall consider presently.

Another answer I have received is, *I have repented of my sins.* The individual who gives this answer is obviously schooled in the gospel, but where are we told we must repent of our sins to be saved? To be sure it is something we should do to maintain a healthy relationship with the Lord, but we are, time and again, told to believe in order to be saved, not to repent. Our *faith* is what gets us to heaven. Should a judge forgive a mass murderer simply because he asks forgiveness? That would be the last case such a judge would preside over! Repentance for our sins is certainly *not* our ticket into heaven, nor should it be! At its root, this is simply another works-based answer to the question of salvation.

A third answer a girl once gave me as to why she should be allowed into heaven was this one: *I believe in Jesus Christ.* I could not for a moment *see* anything wrong with this answer but it *felt* wrong! It took me time to sort through it to discover why. This girl was making a work out of believing. Her response was basically *I'm doing what I need to do to be saved. I am believing in Jesus Christ!* The biblical meaning of the word *believe* was entirely passive, but we have turned belief into an active work which represents our contribution to our salvation, and that, at its root, is entirely incorrect.

The problem with each one of these answers isn't the verb, it is the subject. To the question, *Why should I let you into heaven,* any answer that begins with the words, *because I* is simply wrong! The correct answer to this question begins *because Jesus…* When you start with these words you can hardly go wrong. *Because Jesus died for me. Because Jesus paid my entrance.* The key to my salvation, all 100% of it, is what Jesus did for me. It has nothing to do with anything I have done. Thus, in today's evangelical world, to preach belief or even faith can be a bit misleading because of the non-biblical meanings we have placed on those words. But is there a better term?

Resting in Jesus

Now allow me to share with you a very important passage from Numbers 15.

> **[32] Now while the sons of Israel were in the wilderness, they found a man gathering wood on the Sabbath day. [33] And those who found him gathering wood, brought him to Moses and Aaron and to all the congregation; [34] and they placed him in custody because it had not been decided what should be done to him. [35] Then the LORD said to Moses, "The man must be put to death; all the congregation shall stone him with stones outside the camp." [36] So all the congregation brought him outside the camp and stoned him to death with stones just as the LORD had commanded Moses.**

Now just what does this passage have to do with the topic at hand? Look closely at it. Does it not shock you? Does death not seem a harsh punishment for someone simply working when he isn't supposed to? That is certainly my reaction to it! But throughout history, orthodox Jews have taken this principle of the Sabbath rest so seriously that they have, at times, been willing to allow their enemies to slaughter them rather than to fight on the sacred day. But what exactly does this mean, and why was the punishment so harsh? To put all this in perspective, let us look at Hebrews 3 and 4:

> **[7] Therefore, just as the Holy Spirit says, "TODAY IF YOU HEAR HIS VOICE, [8] DO NOT HARDEN YOUR HEARTS AS WHEN THEY PROVOKED ME, AS ON THE DAY OF TRIAL IN THE WILDERNESS [9] WHERE YOUR FATHERS PUT ME TO THE TEST AND SAW MY WORKS FOR FORTY YEARS. [10] THEREFORE, I WAS ANGRY WITH THIS GENERATION AND SAID, 'THEY ALWAYS GO ASTRAY IN THEIR HEART, AND THEY DID NOT KNOW MY WAYS'; [11] AS I SWORE IN MY ANGER, 'THEY CERTAINLY SHALL NOT ENTER MY REST.'"**
>
> **[12] Take care, brothers and sisters, that there will not be in any one of you an evil, unbelieving heart that falls away from the living God…**
>
> **4 Therefore, we must fear if, while a promise remains of entering His rest, any one of you may seem to have come short of it. [2] For indeed, we have had good news preached to us just as they also did; but the word they heard did not benefit them because they were not united with those who listened with faith. [3] For we who have believed enter that rest, just as He has said, "AS I SWORE IN MY ANGER, THEY CERTAINLY SHALL NOT ENTER MY REST," although His works were finished from the foundation of the world. [4] For He has said somewhere concerning the seventh day: "AND GOD RESTED ON THE SEVENTH DAY FROM ALL HIS WORKS"; [5] and again in this passage, "THEY CERTAINLY SHALL NOT ENTER MY REST." [6] Therefore, since it remains for some to enter it, and those who previously had good news preached to them failed to enter because of disobedience, [7] He again sets a certain day, "Today" saying through David after so long a time just as has been said before, "TODAY IF YOU HEAR HIS VOICE DO NOT HARDEN YOUR HEARTS." [8] For if Joshua had given them rest, He would not have spoken of another day after that. [9] Consequently, there remains a Sabbath rest for the people of God. [10] For the one who has entered His rest has himself also rested from his works as God did from His. [11] Therefore, let's make every effort to enter that rest so that no one will fall by following the same example of disobedience.**

To interpret this passage, we must understand that it quotes a portion of Psalm 95. This psalm makes clear that the mandate to rest on the seventh day as God did was not so much looking back to

Creation as it was looking forward to a final future rest that God had promised. This future rest represented a liberation from the curse of the fall when God had said, *Cursed is the ground because of you; With hard labor you shall eat from it all the days of your life.* (Genesis 3:17) Now instead of hard labor *all* the days of their lives, the Jews would live six days in hard labor and one day of every seven in faith looking forward to the day when they would be freed from the curse altogether. This future rest, in turn, was symbolized by the rest given in the promised land, but while the Psalmist looks back to the Exodus, he makes clear there was still a future rest: *for if Joshua had given them rest, He would not have spoken of another day after that* which the author of Hebrews affirms was fulfilled in Jesus Christ. The key verse here is 4:3, *For we who have believed enter that rest.* Throughout this passage this message screams out loud and clear: *Those who believe, rest!*

Finally consider the words of Jesus in the final three verses of Matthew 11:

> **28 "Come to Me all who are weary and burdened and I will give you rest. 29 Take My yoke upon you and learn from Me for I am gentle and humble in heart and YOU WILL FIND REST FOR YOUR SOULS. 30 For My yoke is comfortable, and My burden is light."**

Once again, *Those who believe rest!* Those who do not rest, it is because they do not believe and have not come to Christ. Those who do not believe, perish in their unbelief. Thus, we understand that the man who broke the Sabbath was killed for his unbelief.

In fin Christians of our day have come to the false conclusion that it is their faith that saves them. While the Bible does speak over and over of the importance of our belief, it is not that belief that saves us. Ephesians 2:8-10 places all in perspective:

> **For by grace you have been saved through faith; and this is not of yourselves, it is the gift of God; 9 not a result of works so that no one may boast. 10 For we are His workmanship created in Christ Jesus for good works which God prepared beforehand so that we would walk in them.**

It is grace that saves us, not faith. Faith is not even something we contribute to the process; the faith through which His grace works, comes as much by grace as our salvation itself. *through faith; and this is not of yourselves, it is the gift of God;* Therefore, we contribute neither works nor even faith to our salvation.

The modern evangelical understanding of faith as our contribution to our salvation is patently false. Thus, I would *not* echo Paul's exhortation to the Philippian jailor *Believe in the Lord Jesus, and you will be saved* because we misinterpret it. I would say rather *rest in the Lord Jesus and you will be saved* because that is what it means to believe. Our young people must be made to understand this. There is nothing they can do, so they might as well stop trying and just rest!

In ironic truth, it is a lot of work to rest. Everything that is within us cries out that we need to earn or at least deserve our salvation. Thus, we want to add to our faith all kinds of works: to attend church, to do good to others, to read our Bibles, all just in case. Still, to add just a small amount of work to our faith, completely undermines that same faith. He who works dies! Faith means putting all of our eggs into one basket and saying, *Lord Jesus, I am going to trust in You and You alone to save me. If it does not please you to save me, then I am lost, but I shall not attempt to add even one small thing to my salvation because I know that he who works stands condemned, and that only he who rests shall enter eternity.*

Now to be sure works are not absent from Christian living. If we continue on to verse 10, we understand that we were created for good works. The difference is *when* we work. An unbeliever works and then rests. A Christian rests and then works. An unbeliever works with the hope that he might be saved and find rest. A Christian rests so that he might then work without fear. In all matters concerning salvation we rest. Then, when we have had the easy yoke of Jesus placed upon us, we begin the good works for which we were created.

But How do I Know?

Now the first step is learning to rest completely in Jesus Christ. However, God is sovereign. How can I know that I am among the elect to begin with? Where is the evidence? This is a question with which many theological Calvinists, giants in the faith, have struggled throughout history. If I do not choose God, but He chooses me, how can I know I'm on His list? This is the first fundamental question a young person raised with the knowledge of Jesus Christ needs an answer to. Second, how do I know I won't *lose* my salvation? The answers to these two questions are key to experiencing true liberation from the tutorage of the law in Jesus Christ and identifying a young person as a true son or daughter of the living God. The answers to both these questions, as we might guess, are found in Romans 8. Let us begin with verses 5 and 6:

> **For those who are in accord with the flesh, set their minds on the things of the flesh, but those who are in accord with the Spirit, the things of the Spirit. ⁶ For the mind set on the flesh is death, but the mind set on the Spirit is life and peace…**

So, a true believer sets his mind on the things of the Spirit. That is to say, he *thinks* about spiritual things. Note, this says nothing of how such a person *acts*. Is it possible that he may commit horrible sins? Paul tells us, just a few verses earlier in chapter 7, how this principle played out in his own life. Consider verses 14-23:

> **For we know that the Law is spiritual, but I am fleshly, sold into bondage to sin. ¹⁵ For I do not understand what I am doing; for I am not practicing what I want to do, but I do the very thing I hate. ¹⁶ However, if I do the very thing I do not want to do, I agree with the Law that the Law is good. ¹⁷ But now no longer am I the one doing it, but sin that dwells in me. ¹⁸ For I know that good does not dwell in me, that is in my flesh; for the willing is present in me, but the doing of the good is not. ¹⁹ For the good that I want, I do not do, but I practice the very evil that I do not want. ²⁰ But if I do the very thing I do not want, I am no longer the one doing it, but sin that dwells in me.**
>
> **²¹ I find then the principle that evil is present in me, the one who wants to do good. ²² For I joyfully agree with the law of God in the inner person ²³ but I see a different law in the parts of my body waging war against the law of my mind and making me a prisoner of the law of sin, the law which is in my body's parts.**

Now the commentators I have consulted are nearly evenly divided as to whether this passage reflects Paul's struggles as a Christian or his struggles previous to coming to Christ. There should be no question. The condition Paul describes, perfectly illustrates the truth he states in 8:5-6. Has Paul not set his mind on the things of the Spirit when he tells us: *For I joyfully agree with the law of God in the inner person?* And yet he lives in conflict with his mind's desire: *For the good that I want, I do not do, but I practice the very evil that I do not want.* By his own test he demonstrates himself to be in accord with the Spirit because of the way he thinks even though he finds himself constantly acting in ways that he abhors.

Here, then, is the answer we seek. If we try to measure our salvation by the way we act, we shall *always* fall short. The measure of our salvation is answered by the question: *What is on your mind?* Do I have that desire to do what pleases God? The very fact that I am interested in such questions is a good indication as to the answer. A true Christian may sin a thousand times, but he shall *never* approve of that sin. The last verse of Romans 1 describes unbelievers in this way: *and although they know the ordinance of God, that those who practice such things are worthy of death, they not only do the same, but also approve of those who practice them.* A Christian may well do these things, but he will never approve of those who practice them. The mark of a true Christian is that he hates the sin he finds within himself. An unbeliever never experiences such a conflict, as his mind as well as his body are set on the things of the flesh.

Thus, we answer the first question. We may know that we are saved when we think on the things of the Spirit. But what about the second? How can we know that we will never lose our salvation? Of course, up to a point we have already answered this question. If our salvation depends at all upon us, then we have no hope at all, and if we have nothing to contribute to gaining our salvation to begin with, how can we believe we might have some responsibility in retaining it? And if we are not responsible for retaining our salvation, would we accuse *God* of fickleness in that we question our security? However, Romans 8 gives us another solid evidence that our destiny is secure. The last two verses of that chapter say:

For I am convinced that neither death, nor life, nor angels, nor principalities, nor things present, nor things to

come, nor powers, [39] nor height, nor depth, nor any other created thing will be able to separate us from the love of God that is in Christ Jesus our Lord.

Now here is the key: *Nor things to come… will be able to separate us from the love of God that is in Christ Jesus our Lord.* Is not the future what we fear by even asking this question? *I know I'm saved today, but what if I really mess up tomorrow?* We can be assured that nothing in the future will be able to separate us from Christ's love. Nothing that I might do shall separate me from Christ's love. Christ's blood is sufficient, not only to *save* me, but to *keep* me until that day when I see Him face to face!

Not My Own

Once a young person has come to Christ, the question must arise, *Now what?* The answer would take a lifetime to study, and it is not my purpose to give a complete discipleship guide here, but a young person must at least understand that there *is* a *Now what.* He must know that the gospel is not simply a fire insurance policy designed merely to preserve him from hell. It is not only relevant to the moment of his death; it is intended to give form to his entire life. We are not meant to keep resting for the rest of eternity. What meaning would our lives hold if we did?

So just what does this look like biblically? The last two verses of 1 Corinthians 6 say:

> **Or do you not know that your body is a temple of the Holy Spirit within you whom you have from God and *that* you are not your own? [20] For you have been bought for a price: therefore, glorify God in your body.**

Now the immediate context of this verse is sexual sin, but the principle goes far deeper. Young person, now that you have come to Christ, you are not your own any longer. You were bought with a price, and, belonging to another, you now answer to that other. You are a slave of Jesus Christ.

And Jesus expands on this concept of having bought us with a price with these two, one-verse parables in Matthew 13:

> **44 "The kingdom of heaven is like a treasure hidden
> in the field which a man found and hid *again*; and from joy
> *over it* he goes and sells everything that he has and buys that
> field.
> 45 "Again the kingdom of heaven is like a merchant
> seeking fine pearls, 46 and upon finding one pearl of great
> value, he went and sold everything that he had and bought it.**

Now a treasure undiscovered is no treasure at all. It becomes a treasure in the hands of him who values it. Many times, these verses have been interpreted such that the believer is the merchant who sells everything to buy the treasure, but the truth is, we have given nothing to obtain that treasure. Jesus, in fact, found a lump of coal in the field and went and sold all he had in order to buy that field and that lump of coal because Jesus knows how to turn lumps of coal into diamonds! He was willing to pay everything, including His own life, to obtain that hidden, tarnished treasure which He knew He could make shine.

But is it good to be a slave? Consider the words of the Queen of Sheba:

> **It was a true story that I heard in my own land about
> your words and your wisdom. 7 But I did not believe the stories
> until I came and my *own* eyes saw *it all*. And behold the half
> *of it* was not reported to me. You have exceeded *in* wisdom
> and prosperity the report which I heard. 8 Blessed are your
> men, *and* blessed are these servants of yours who stand before
> you continually *and* hear your wisdom!**

While our historical understanding of slavery makes the very word repugnant to our ears, the fact is that being a slave of a great master can be a glorious thing. If the servants of Solomon were blessed to stand in his presence, how much more slaves of Jesus Christ which He Himself bought at so great a price!

Furthermore, slavery to Jesus Christ is not so much of a demand as it is an invitation. It is entirely an act of voluntarily submitting our will to His. Let us look once again at that passage we cited earlier in this chapter from the end of Matthew 11:

> **28 "Come to Me all who are weary and burdened and
> I will give you rest. 29 Take My yoke upon you and learn from**

Me, for I am gentle and humble in heart, and YOU WILL FIND REST FOR YOUR SOULS. [30] **For My yoke is comfortable, and My burden is light."**

In this passage Jesus invites us to two different things. We studied the first in that previous section. He invites us to come to Him that He might give us rest. Then in verse 29 is the second invitation, and I do not believe that this is just a renaming of the first. Now Jesus invites us to *Take My yoke upon you and learn from me…*First, we come to Him, and once we have rested, we take His yoke upon us which gives rest for our souls. First, we are invited to come to Him, and now we are invited to live for Him. We are assured that, *My yoke is comfortable and My burden is light.* Now this is a life-long commitment to present ourselves as living sacrifices, giving up all our futile carnal passions in order to follow Him so that we might become instruments to glorify God.

A common failure within the Church is to simply stop with the first invitation. However, our young people need to understand this commitment. They need to receive this second calling as much as the first. If Christ's calling means nothing more than giving me security of salvation, then the fact that I am saved soon becomes very dull, and new Christians may become discouraged with their new-found faith.

Consider the lives of Jesus' disciples: Peter, Andrew, James, John, Philip, and Nathanael. These men experienced the first calling in John chapter 1 where John the Baptist pointed Jesus out to them as the Lamb of God. From that point on, they followed Jesus without any particular obligation or commitment. They were there when He changed water to wine at the wedding in Cana. They were there when He celebrated the Passover in Jerusalem and drove out the moneychangers from the temple. (He did this a second time in the last week of His life.) They were also there and saw Him performing miracles at the Temple. They were close by when Jesus had his interview with Nicodemus. They also saw when He ministered to the Samaritan woman at the well on the way back to Galilee.

These disciples received the second calling after the miraculous catch of fish when Jesus told them, *Follow Me and I will make you Fishers of Men.* They already believed in Him. They had already found rest from their lifelong search. It was then that Jesus called them to take His yoke upon them and learn from Him. It was then that He called them to lifelong commitment.

It is important to note, we do not become slaves of Jesus Christ because He needs slaves. Most slave masters in the world *need* their slaves for one reason or another, to do something they cannot do themselves. Jesus needs nothing and no one. He is perfectly capable of doing all He purposes without any help from any of His creatures. Jesus didn't need Peter and company; they needed Him as Peter so clearly recognized when he fell at the Lord's feet pleading *Go away from me Lord, for I am a sinful man!*

In the same way our young people need to hear that second calling to submit and commit their lives to Him. Yes, Jesus does place a yoke on our shoulders and a burden on our back, but that yoke is comfortable and that burden is light, and it is that yoke and that burden that give meaning to our otherwise meaningless lives. It is through that yoke and that burden that we realize our ultimate purpose, as 1 Corinthians 6:20 says, of glorifying God in our bodies. Yes, to die *is* gain, but to live is Christ!

Running without Growing Weary

Have you ever seen God? Most of us who have lived in the Lord for many years can point to one or several occasions in which God entered our lives in a dramatic and unquestionable fashion such that we could never doubt again, but most of the young people of our schools have not had that experience. Job is a case study of a man who had never before met God.

Job is a poetic, not a historical book, and there exists very little evidence to suggest that he ever really existed, but the book teaches us how to proceed when the world is falling down around us. In the first two chapters, Job, who is a very wealthy and respected man, suddenly sees his entire world fall down around him. First, he loses his entire fortune and all ten of his beloved children. Then even his health is stripped away such that he sits in ashes and scrapes his raw skin with broken pieces of pottery, an outcast from society rejected by even his wife. For the next 30 chapters of the book, Job and his three friends, followed by a fourth friend in chapters 33-37, struggle to find meaning to the horrible trials he has faced. His friends insist that he must have sinned, but Job staunchly maintains his innocence. In chapter 19, after a long description of his many sufferings, he cries out in verses 25-27:

> **Yet as for me, I know that my Redeemer lives, And at the last He will take His stand on the earth. [26] Even after my skin is destroyed, Yet from my flesh I will see God [27] Whom I, on my part, shall behold for myself, And *whom* my eyes will see and not another.**

I will see God! What a magnificent hope and confidence Job expressed in that beautiful sentence! Somehow, Job foresaw the end from the beginning, and it gave him the strength to cling to his integrity and deflect every one of the relentless attacks of Satan. And how does the story end? Job got exactly what he expected. God came in a whirlwind and spoke a long time not giving him one answer to any of the questions he had wrestled with, but presenting Himself in all His majesty as the supreme governor of all Creation. After God's long discourse, Job finally answers at the beginning of chapter 42:

> **"I know that You can do all things, And that no plan is impossible for You. [3] 'Who is this, who conceals advice without knowledge?' Therefore, I have declared that which I did not understand, Things too wonderful for me which I do not know. [4] 'Please listen, and I will speak; I will ask You and You instruct me.' [5] I have heard of You by the hearing of the ear; But now my eye sees You; [6] Therefore, I retract, And I repent sitting on dust and ashes."**

Were all Job's sufferings worthwhile? In the end he saw God! He saw his Redeemer in the flesh in exactly the way that he had hoped. Certainly, in a way, God need not have spoken a single word. Simply a glimpse of the Almighty was enough to quiet all his fears and raise his faith to the point that he would never doubt again. Before that, God was only someone that he had heard about, but now God was someone whom he knew personally. Now he had more than just a book knowledge of God; He had a personal testimony, and his life would never again be the same. The book of Revelation states of the brethren who overcome: *And they overcame him because of the blood of the Lamb and because of the word of their testimony...* By two things we overcome by the blood of the Lamb, what God did two thousand years ago for us, and by the word of our testimony, what God has done in our own lives right here during our time on earth.

In my case, I can point to three very specific miracles in which the Lord has touched me in a very personal and profound way such as to change the entire direction of my life which I shall share in the final chapter of this book. Many other mature Christians could point to such times in their own lives, but most of our children cannot. We must encourage them with the word of our own testimony. The day will surely come when they too shall see Jesus. Until that time, we must exhort them to continue the struggle based on the things they have heard as Job did, hoping for the day when they too shall see their Redeemer. The reward is simply too great to do otherwise!

XI. Now my Eyes See You

The first time that God intervened in my life in a miraculously personal way was when I was 15 years old. I had been a believer since I was old enough to think, but I could not get past my need for works to go along with the blood of Jesus. I lived in a constant awareness of my own mortality and a terror of hell. I would cyclically pass through periods when my waking moments were constantly haunted with the specter of that awful final destination I was not at all sure I wouldn't one day see.

My early sophomore year of high school was simultaneously one of the highlights and one of the lowlights of my life. It was a highlight because I was thoroughly enjoying myself. I had been admitted to the elite swing choir at my school which was one of the best in the state and produced several professional musicians. The choir was composed of 18 members of which 11 were seniors. I was the only sophomore male in the group. For a young 15-year-old, it was the pinnacle of artistic success and put me in a place where I began to bloom socially, particularly with the girls who had previously terrified me.

It was a lowlight spiritually. Now I had always been a model student in both school and Sunday school. This had not changed, but spiritually, I had withered away on the inside to the point I found myself incapable of reading the Bible and at night, when I went to bed, my mind wandered so badly I couldn't concentrate for even 30 seconds on prayer. Probably a lot of it had to do with sexual fantasies that dominated my every waking moment. No one else knew of that, but even sitting at school or even church apparently listening to the teacher or preacher, my mind was completely immersed in the basest of fantasies. To make matters worse, I had completely lost my fear of hell. No longer did I cower in terror at the thought of being eternally separated from my Maker even though such a scenario now seemed more likely than ever. Still, the fact that this did not concern me *did* concern me a great deal. Every night I forced myself to say a single, one-lined prayer before sinking into my fantasies. *Lord bring me back!*

The Lord answered that prayer when I went to a music festival along with several other members of my choir the last weekend in October, 1981. After a long day of rehearsal for the performance the following day, we stayed in a hotel that night where the supervision was non-existent. I was in a room with three other young men. Some of the young people were drinking. The girls were in and out of our room until the wee hours of the morning. One was still there when, finally, one of my roommates decided it was time to shut off the lights and told her to go back to her room. She said she would just spend the night with us. "All right!" he said and shut off the lights and climbed into the queen size bed with her in between him and his bunkmate.

I'm sure now that there was very little possibility of any sexual activity occurring in that bed, but, in my naivety, this was the moral fall of the century. Or maybe I am naïve now. At any rate, I was alarmed and began doing something I hadn't done in months. I started to pray. I prayed that God would give me the words to persuade them to get her out of the room. I prayed and prayed, formulated a plan and broke the silence to display my persuasive eloquence. They all laughed and ridiculed me. I started praying again and again I came up with some other brilliant argument. I got the same reaction. Some three or four times I repeated this folly. Finally, I understood that nothing I might say would have any effect, so I turned to God and said, "Lord these people aren't going to listen to me no matter what I say. But I want her out of this room, and I am going to pray to You for the rest of this night, if necessary, until she leaves." I fully expected to lie in my bed for the short rest of the night praying, but in that very moment—not a second later—the voice of the guy she was with broke the silence, "L____ don't you think it's about time you went back to your room? I listened with baited breath as they got up, put on their shoes, and he walked her over to her room.

As simple as it seems, that night changed my life. I went to bed again silently praising God. As far as I thought I had strayed from Him, He had never left my side. In the silence of that dark hotel room, God formally recognized me as His beloved son and took away the tutor of the law. It was the closest I have ever come to a conversion experience. I have never again doubted my salvation and never again been terrorized by the fires of hell. I have experienced the full joy of a child of God! Before that day I had only heard of God, but that day, I saw Him with my own eyes, and my life has never been the same!

After high school I went to Purdue University and received a bachelor's of science in chemical engineering. My faith steadily grew and matured. By the time I graduated, I perceived myself to have arrived at a state pretty close to perfection before God. I would not have said that, of course, even to myself, but it is how I felt. I was following Him to the best of my ability and had a great relationship with Him, praying and studying the Bible constantly. I was involved directly in several different ministries within and outside my church. I had a great relationship with everyone I knew, as well. I wasn't really aware of any major sins in my life. Things were just great, until…

It was about that time, a year or so after graduating and starting work with Bethlehem Steel on the Indiana lake shore, that God called me into the mission field. I don't remember how it first happened. I don't believe it came from any external event in particular. I just felt strongly that God wanted me to go and that call revealed something ugly in me. I did not have the faith to respond! It was a rude awakening, and it showed me a picture of myself I did not like. While my job was definitely not my dream job, I earned a good living and lived close enough to family and friends to visit often. I was comfortable both economically and socially, and I liked being comfortable. Further, I really desired to be married and couldn't imagine finding a wife in some foreign context. To go to the mission field was to give all that up, and I just was not ready to do that.

It was around Christmas time of 1991, a year and a half after I graduated from college, when I finally humbled myself before God in prayer. *Lord, I just don't have the faith to do this. If You want me to go to the mission field, then you will have to give me another, smaller challenge, so I can step up in faith.* I had no idea what such a challenge might look like. I was really ready to do about anything as long as it didn't require me to leave my job, so I wasn't sure that there *were* any such challenges out there, but that was God's problem not mine. And God indeed knew how to solve it. Within a week of that prayer, my pastor called me up and asked me to consider taking into my apartment a recovering homosexual who had just come to Christ.

Back at that time, that was a much bigger challenge than it would be today, as homosexuality was still seen as unsavory by society as a whole. I was floored by the creative and prompt way in which He had answered my prayer. For the second time in my life, I saw God as certainly as if He had been standing in front of me in physical form. In the end, I really didn't even need the challenge, I just needed to see God answer my prayer. That was enough! I was ready to follow Him to the mission field to wherever He might lead.

Nevertheless, the young man did move in with me, and shortly afterward, he was diagnosed with HIV, a much scarier disease at that time than it is today. He lived with me for nearly two years and taught me many things. I, in turn, did everything I could to strengthen him through his struggles, all the while making my secret preparations to leave for the mission field. In the process, God spoke to me through three very significant scriptures. One was 1 Corinthians 10:13: *No temptation has overtaken you except what is common to humanity. God is faithful, and He will not allow you to be tempted beyond what you are able, but with the temptation, He will also provide a way of escape so that you are able to bear it.* The mission field was a frightening place! But God would not ask anything of me that He would not give me the strength to handle. Romans 8:18 says: *For I consider that the sufferings of this present time are not worth comparing with the glory that is going to be revealed to us.* This verse kept me focused on heaven. However horrible my suffering might be on the mission field in a worst-case scenario, there was something that was incomparably bigger and better than I was even capable of imagining. The third verse was also from Romans 8 verse 28: *We know that all things work together for the good of those who love God: those who are called according to His purpose.* Good would surely come of my obedience to Him. So God would strengthen me to handle anything that might come; as bad as things might get, they could never compare to heaven; and nothing I did would be in vain. God would work. Armed with these three truths, I asked Him for one more thing before committing my life to the mission field. I asked Him for a two-week work trip to see the field first hand wherever in the world He might like to send me.

All through 1992, I searched for a suitable mission trip to take and finally found one with Kids Alive International to the Dominican Republic in March of 1993. When I took that trip, I began to confess to my fellow team members for the first time something that I had kept entirely to myself before that—that I was there seeking God's will as to going into the mission field. Amazingly, at that very time, God gave me the desire of my heart. I met a beautiful Dominican girl who was the first teacher at the brand-new school for at-risk children we had gone to help build. By the end of that trip, God had not only confirmed my calling, but He had given me a woman to share my life and work. The one thing I had thought I would be giving up, God gave me on the mission field even before I officially arrived. Milagros and I have now been married for 26 years and have three children. We have been working all that time at the same school that I helped build the walls for. We have never looked back!

Living on the mission field has been a humbling experience. When I first arrived, I imagined God *needed* me to share His Word with the lost. I now understand that He doesn't need me at all. Had I never answered His call, there isn't one child who would be condemned to hell as a result. God just would have used someone else, and someone else would have received the reward. God sent me to the Dominican Republic because it was here that He wanted to mold and prepare me for that day when I will see Him in glory. He has done that in so many ways, but the greatest of those, in my eyes, was the third time I was privileged to *see* Him. It happened through our financial crisis of 2015!

In truth, we had already been living on the edge for about two years. We just weren't bringing in enough money to pay our salary, and the balance in our reserve was constantly below zero. The mission had to borrow from other accounts to pay us. While we *were* in debt, our incoming donations seemed stable for a long time, and the debt never grew to the point it seemed unmanageable. There were even a couple of times we actually rose out of debt for a month or so. But when 2015 hit, all that turned around, and in the wrong direction. Finishing up 2014, though our debt had risen over the last few months I was hoping for our usual December bounce. It didn't happen! We continued seeing a steady drop, further and further into negative territory through the opening months of 2015 by an average of around $500 a month.

For me, the whole matter provoked a theological crisis. It seemed I could just not take God at His word. *You said, God, "Seek first the kingdom of God and His righteousness and all these things shall be added to you. I think I'm doing that. Why aren't You providing then? Oh, we are not going hungry, and we have clothes on our backs and adequate shelter, but we're doing it on someone else's dime and that just doesn't seem like a proper fulfillment of Your promise. What's up with that?* I felt abandoned by God and ashamed among the office of my mission.

I even wondered, for a while, if God weren't leading us away from the field, but I remembered an illustration I'd heard of John chapter 10. In Israel there was once a guide explaining the passage of the Good Shepherd to his tour group. *The Israeli shepherd always goes out front and leads the sheep,* he explained. *He never drives them from behind.* At that point in the story the bus drove by a large farm where they saw a shepherd doing exactly what the guide had just said shepherds didn't do—driving the sheep from behind. The guide had no answer for this anomaly, so they stopped the bus to question the shepherd. *It's true,* said the shepherd, *that the shepherd leads, rather than drives, the sheep, but I am a butcher, not the shepherd.* As I contemplated that story, I knew that God was not leading me away from the mission field by this crisis. That would have been too much like a butcher driving from behind. My God should be out front calling me to follow!

Finally, I came to a decision. Once, I had tried, for a full year. to raise support and not raised a single dime. Then, God had supplied a new significant supporter from someone I didn't even know. I had also read books about people who just refused to raise support and relied completely on prayer, like Brother Andrew, Hudson Taylor, and George Mueller. Finally, I talked to my wife about the situation and suggested. *Let's not tell anyone what is happening. Let's just pray about it from now through December and see what God will do.* If He didn't act by then, we would have some tough decisions to make! We could not continue to burden the mission forever! My hope was just to get out of debt. I had learned, by then, that God did not usually give us more than we needed, and I had learned not to pray for it. *I don't care if we have ten dollars extra!* I told God, *I just don't want to be in debt anymore!*

Well, we hit our all-time low of over $5600 in debt in May. In June we received a quarterly bump but the general trend continued through both June and July. Awaiting our August report, which I expected would drop us close to $7000 in debt, we met with an older missionary couple just so they could stand by us and help us pray and work through the situation as it developed. Then, a few days later, we got our first bit of good news. Our August statement showed four thousand dollars of unexpected donations and those from five or six different people. Our debt was cut in half. Still, we were far from out of the woods.

At that point the mission administration finally called with a mind to work on our situation giving us a detailed plan of action which included them sending a letter to our supporters. I explained the decision my wife and I had made and asked them not to send the letter until after Christmas. We continued to wait upon the Lord. The month of September also showed another $4000 of unexpected donations, and we were out of debt for the first time in well over a year. Then, in October, the mission called to tell me we had received a $10,000 anonymous donation. In the months of November and December, we received another seven or eight thousand dollars of unexpected donations finishing the year at $16500 positive, a swing of $22,000 since our low point in May. This huge surplus gave me confidence to ask for my first pay raise in five years which, with two kids in college, we desperately needed. The Lord supplied all that excess, far more than I asked for, in order to give me that confidence to ask for a raise that He knew I would need.

Why did God ever allowed us to fall so low? To me it is crystal clear now. He had to vanquish all hope in anyone or anything outside of Himself because He was unwilling to share His glory. Otherwise, we would easily have given credit to earthly things. If we had received only one or two very large, unexpected donations we might have chalked it up to coincidence, but God provided us with at least ten or twelve. Nor would we have appreciated it if we had decided to launch a big support raising campaign ourselves. Beyond that, God gave us a testimony to share with our mission, which typically takes a much more aggressive approach to fundraising, and with others around us who might be going through similar struggles—or maybe even with someone on the other side of the world who had never even heard our names.

Months after our financial miracle, I was sitting at the home of a college friend who told us an amazing story: The ministry of the Indian chapter for a well-known international mission was in dyer straights. They had had a field director who had run the ministry economically into the ground. I don't know if the man had actually robbed the mission or if he had just been an extremely poor administrator, but either way, the mission was in trouble. Now they had a new field director charged with picking up the pieces. He worked hard to raise finances but was unsuccessful. Many of the old donors had abandoned them and even the home office in the United States was tired of the monkey business and offered little help. The poor man didn't know where to turn, but he wrote a letter to some of his supporters including a friend of his near Indianapolis who was a friend of my friend's. One day over coffee the two women were chatting and my friend heard of the situation in India. Having just received our prayer letter about the miraculous way God had met our needs, she pulled it out and shared it with her friend. Intrigued, that woman in turn passed it to the director of the Indian mission. That gentleman read it and figured he had nothing to lose. He called his staff together and informed them that all fund-raising efforts were to stop and the entire staff was just cry out to the Lord for His provision. I do not know the details, but within a short time the mission had left its financial problems behind. As my friend told me this story I was absolutely floored! How amazing God is!

Now with eyes of faith I can see many other ways in which the Lord has worked throughout my life. He has done many smaller miracles such as the time he caused me to misplace some money within my own house and find it many months later in exactly the moment when I saw no hope of making it through until my next paycheck. He has spoken to me through his Word so many times that I could not begin to count them, but these three great miracles are the ones that have truly opened my spiritual eyes. I am naturally somewhat of a Thomas, doubting anything people tell me until I see it for myself, and for this I do not apologize. Despite the Lord's rebuke of that disciple, it seems to me that one should *not* easily believe that someone has risen from the dead and *should* demand proof. Those who do believe such a thing so easily might justly be called naïve or credulous. After all, how many people do you know that have done it? It's not quite the same thing as being asked to believe that someone had steak for dinner last night or traveled to Europe last summer. On the other hand, we, unlike Thomas, have generations of witnesses to attest to the fact that the crucified Jesus Christ is alive, many of whom gave their own lives rather than deny it, including Thomas himself whom, we are told was run through by a brahmin's spear in India. We may rest in these to fortify our faith until the day when Jesus gives us testimony of our own.

What is your story? Have you told your students about the times you have seen Jesus with your own eyes? They need to hear it. After all, the Bible is just full of old stories and legends, until the day that you discover that they are *not* just old stories and legends. Perhaps your testimony shall be the one that causes your students, like Job, to cling to what they hear until that day in which they too behold the Lord with their own eyes and repent in dust and ashes!

Sources

To write a formal bibliography for this work would be somewhat of a challenge as most of my sources have been trainings rather than actual books. However, I wish, as much as possible, to give credit to whom credit is due.

The primary and by far the most important source of this work, other than the Bible itself, is the training conferences of the Faith Biblical Counseling Ministries of Faith Church from Lafayette, IN. They put on a six-track biblical counseling training every year in Lafayette and in many other places around the U.S. and the world. I have taken tracks 1 and 3 and cannot say how much they have enriched me. While I do not often cite these trainings throughout this book, the simple fact is that they underlie virtually every word. It is not an exaggeration to say that this book would not exist without them.

Another fundamental source of all I have written are the many works of Jay Adams. His books are foundational for the trainings presented by Faith Church, and, after having been inspired by those trainings, I have devoured a great number of his numerous works as well. Once again, I seldom cite him directly, but as he underlies all the teachings I received from Faith Counseling Ministries, so also he underlies nearly everything I have written. His works, *Competent to Counsel,* and *A Christian Counselor's Handbook,* are his two must reads. However, I have quoted in my introduction from *Lectures on Counseling* page 11 for which I shall write out a complete Bibliography below.

A secondary source I have cited is Ken Sande. While Ken is the head of the Peacemakers ministries and has written the book, *Peacemakers,* which contains some fundamental counseling tools, his work that directly affects this book is his on-line training course of Relational Wisdom. Everything that I cite from him is taken from that training.

Another secondary source I have cited is Paul David Tripp. The material of his I have used comes from a series of lectures entitled *Your Christian School: A Culture of Grace?*

With this said and done I shall list in Bibliographical form the four books that serve as direct reference for this present work.

Adams, Jay E., *Lectures on Counseling,* Grand Rapids, MI, Zondervan, 1977.

Greene, Ross W., *Lost at School,* New York, NY, Scribner, 2014

Kellemen, Robert W., *Gospel-Centered Counseling,* Grand Rapids, MI., 2014

Kellemen, Robert W., *Gospel Conversations,* Grand Rapids, MI., 2015

Index of Scriptural References

About the Author

Kerry Dougan was born in 1966 in the small town of Madison, Indiana. He was raised in a Christian home with one younger brother. He received his bachelor's of science in chemical engineering from Purdue University in 1989. After spending nearly six years working at the Bethlehem Steel mill on the Indiana Lakeshore, he felt the call to the mission field. On an exploratory trip to the Dominican Republic, he met his wife Milagros, a native Dominican. The two were married a year later in 1994 and returned to the Dominican as full-time missionaries in 1995 after the birth of their first child. They have now been working as a couple in a school for at risk children in Jarabacoa, in the mountains of the central Dominican Republic for twenty-five years under the auspices of the child sponsorship organization, Kids Alive International. They have three adult children, Sarah, Oliver , and Alina.

Kerry's interest in the Bible has been innate since he was a small child when he would spend his entire Saturdays immersed in the Scriptures. He has written two other books, those on biblical prophecy, *The Vultures' End; Death is Swallowed up in Victory,* a commentary on biblical prophecy, and a novel called *Journey to the Edge of Time.*

You may contact the author at the E-mail kdougandr@yahoo.com or at his missionary mail service:

Kerry Dougan
Unit 3049 KAIDR
3170 Airmans Drive
Fort Pierce, FL 34946

Information about Kids Alive International about sponsoring a child through that organization or supporting the Dougans in their work in the Dominican Republic may be found at www.kidsalive.org